MAKING PICTURES OF WAR

REALIA ET IMAGINARIA IN THE ICONOLOGY OF THE ANCIENT NEAR EAST

Edited by

Laura Battini

ARCHAEOPRESS ANCIENT NEAR EASTERN ARCHAEOLOGY 1

ARCHAEOPRESS PUBLISHING LTD
Gordon House
276 Banbury Road
Oxford OX2 7ED

www.archaeopress.com

ISBN 978 1 78491 403 5
ISBN 978 1 78491 404 2 (e-Pdf)

© Archaeopress and the individual authors 2016

Cover: VICTORY STELE OF NARAMSIN. AKKADIAN PERIOD. LOUVRE MUSEUM

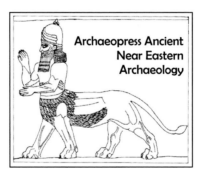

Archaeopress Ancient Near Eastern Archaeology

Printed in England by Oxuniprint, Oxford
This book is available direct from Archaeopress or from our website www.archaeopress.com

Contents

List of Figures iii

Abbreviations and General References vii
   Abbreviations vii
   References ix

Acknowledgments x

Introduction: the War and its Representations 1
Laura Battini
   References 3

Some Observations on the War Scenes on the Seals from Mari City II 5
Dominique Beyer
   The seals of King Ishqi-Mari 5
   The seal of *Shakkanakku* Iddin-Eshtar 12
   References 12

Elements of War Iconography at Mari 13
Béatrice Muller
   Graphic vocabulary: components of the military apparatus 13
   Costumes and weapons 13
      Costumes and weapons from City II (DA III-b) 13
      Costumes and weapons from City III 15
      Heavy equipment: harnesses 16
      Frame 17
      The figure of the vanquished enemy 19
   Elements of iconographic syntax 19
      Soldier and prisoner 19
      Clues about a military hierarchy from shell inlays 20
      Warriors and the image of the victorious King in the Old Babylonian period 22
      The axe, the javelin and the bow 22
   Overall compositions and significance – the place of Mari in war iconography 25
      Overall composition of the mosaic shell panels: new paths 25
      Mari and the modalities of the royal victory iconography in the Old Babylonian period .. 25
   Conclusion 26
   References 27

Visualizing War in the Old Babylonian Period:
Drama and Canon 29
Silvana Di Paolo
   Victories and Defeats: The Sedimentation of War Experiences 29
   'Inscribing' the War on the Bodies between Aberrations and Tangible Signs 31
   The Power of Symbols: the 'Canon' of Naram-Sin 33
   References 35

Middle Assyrian Drama in Depicting War: a Step towards Neo-Assyrian Art 37
Laura Battini
   The grammar of Middle Assyrian depictions of war 37
   Outline of a syntax 40
   Relationships with the Iron Age 41
   References 42

"Losing One's Head". Some Hints on Procedures and Meanings of Decapitation in the Ancient Near East 45
Rita Dolce

    The act of decapitation 46
    The act of displaying 47
    Destinations of the SH: some pieces of evidence 50
    The moving SH 52
    References 54
    Abstract 56
    Key words: 56

Where is the Public? A New Look at the Brutality Scenes in Neo-Assyrian Royal Inscriptions and Art 57
Ariel Bagg

    Introduction 57
    Catalogue of atrocities: The written sources 58
        Group A: Soldiers 58
        Group B: Members of the elite 58
        Group C: Civilians 60
    The audience of the royal inscriptions 60
    Catalogue of atrocities: The iconographic sources 62
        Group A: Soldiers 62
        Group B: Elite Members 62
        Group C: Civilians 63
    The audience of the palace reliefs 65
    The brutality scenes in their context 68
    Conclusions 71
    References 71
    Appendix: Catalogue of brutality scenes in Neo-Assyrian art 72

Images of War in the Assyrian Period: What They Show and What They Hide 83
Davide Nadali

    References 87

List of Figures

Some Observations on the War Scenes on the Seals from Mari City II

Figure 1.1: Schematic Diagram of the North Part of P-1 with the Positions of the Sigillographic Finds. 6

Figure 1.2: Door Seal with Imprints of *Version a* of Ishqi-Mari's Seal. 7

Figure 1.3: Fragmentary Imprint of *Version a* of Ishqi-Mari's Seal. 7

Figure 1.4: Graphic Reconstruction of the Imprint of *Version a*. 7

Figure 1.5: Door Seal with Fragmentary Imprints of *Version b* of Ishqi-Mari's Seal. 8

Figure 1.6: Fragmentary Imprint of *Version b*. 8

Figure 1.7: Fragmentary Imprint: Upper Section of *Version b*. 8

Figure 1.8: Fragmentary Imprint: King Ishqi-Mari (*Version b*) 9

Figure 1.9: Graphic Reconstruction of the Imprint of *Version b* (2007) 9

Figure 1.10: Graphic Reconstruction of the Imprint of *Version b*: New Version. 10

Figure 1.11: Door Seal with Fragmentary Imprints of Iddin-Eshtar's Seal. 11

Figure 1.12: Fragmentary Imprints of the Seal of Iddin-Eshtar and the Seal of a King Iku-X. 11

Figure 1.13: Graphic Reconstruction of the Imprint of Iddin-Eshtar's Seal. 11

Elements of War Iconography at Mari

Figure 2.1: Inlaid mother-of-pearl from the Temple of Ninni-zaza (Mari, City II) : helmeted soldiers. H. average 4.5-5cm. a - Parrot 1952: fig. 66. b - Drawing of a selection of parts. Parrot 1967: 209-214, fig. 252-254 (cf. pl. LXIII). 14

Figure 2.2: Plaque of gypsum or alabaster M. 4989-5029-5045 from room 46 of pseudo-Palace (Mari, City II) : scene of siege (?) (fragmentary?). H. 16cm ; l. 9.8cm. Parrot 1974: fig. 30. 15

Figure 2.3: Terracotta stamped plaques from the Great Royal Palace (Mari, City III) : soldier with a long weapon (spear?) and an axe. a - M. 768, room 62 (near the Throne Room 65, official sector M). Parrot 1959: fig. 55 et cf. pl. XXIX. b - M. 1073, court 87 (sector G : chambers of the staff belonging to the King's House). Parrot 1959: pl. XXIX. 15

Figure 2.4: Fragments of mural painting from room 220' (sector F: royal private apartments on the first floor) of Great Royal Palace (Mari, City III). a - M. 4596 : archer standing at rest. H. 31cm. Gouache J. Depauw, © MAM, slide A. Parrot. b - M. 4592 : end of a building in bricks bordered by a fragmentary character (*polos* and shoulder) dressed in a blue and white striped garment. H. 12cm. 16

Figure 2.5: Fragments of mural painting from the West wall of the Court 106 (official sector M) of the Great Royal Palace (Mari, City III) : figure of victorious King (module 1, restored h. c.1.60m). Parrot 1958: fig. 35 and 36. a - Elements of garment with rich drapes having scalloped edge, a dagger in a side. b - Folded arm, hand gripping a tuft of hair belonging likely to two individuals. c - Provisional restitution. Muller 2008, never published. 17

Figure 2.6: Graffiti engraved with a point on plaster (*juss*) of a wall of room 52 (sector H, chambers of the staff belonging to the Women's House) of the Great Royal Palace (Mari, City III) : soldiers. Parrot 1958: fig. 13 and 14. a - Bearded and helmeted soldier who is about to launch a weapon like a dagger or a sword rather than a feature weapon. Preserved H. of the character: 14cm. b - Profile heads of two characters, one with a flat headgear, the other with an helmet. Preserved H. c. 8cm and 10cm. 18

Figure 2.7: Piece of inlaid mother-of-pearl from space 4 of the pseudo-Palace (Mari, City II) : deck tank showing a pair of engraved reins in its upper indentation ; the lower edge curved leaves room for the installation of a wheel. H. 6.8cm. Never published © MAM J.-Cl. Margueron. 18

Figure 2.8: Piece of inlaid mother-of-pearl from space 20 (square) south of the Temple of Ishtar (Mari, City II) and belonging to the Standard: fragmentary wheel associated with the box of a chariot on whose step the legs of a soldier brace themselves. Total h.: c. 7cm. © B. Muller. Louvre AO 17572/19820. 18

Figure 2.9: Miniature registry of fragmentary mural paintings from room 220' (sector F: royal private apartments on first floor) of Great Royal Palace (Mari, City III). a – Head caped with a *polos* blue and white striped. (M. 4587) at the corner of a brick building. H. of the fragment 10.9cm. © MAM, slide A. Parrot. b - Restitution of register. Muller 1990: pl. XXVIII p. 554........ 19

Figure 2.10: Piece of inlaid mother-of-pearl M. 2477 from room 13 of the temple of Ninni-zaza (Mari, City II) : Kneeling prisoner. H. 7cm. Parrot 1952: fig. 67. 20

Figure 2.11: Pieces of Standard from space 20 (square) south of the temple of Ishtar (Mari, City II). A - bust of the military dignitary M. 474 *in situ*, yet in connection with the background and border, while the bottom of the garment is visible above on the plate. Parrot 1956: detail of fig. 32. B - Restitution by Parrot (1956: PL. LVIIa) 21

Figure 2.12: Fragment of the panel inlaid from the passage 52/49 of the pseudo-Palace of City II, level P-1: helmeted soldier pushing a prisoner (M. 4785 and M. 4793) and wearing clothes of this one on the top of his javelin which is pointed downward. H. of the character c. 8.5cm. Parrot 1969: figures 12 and 13. a - Outlook *in situ*. b - Restitution of a set as presented in the Museum of Damascus. 22

Figure 2.13: Contour of warrior M. 471 (temple of Ishtar, Standard) by comparison with the previous figure. 23

Figure 2.14: Fragmentary mural painting from room 220' (sector F: royal private apartments on the first floor) of the Great Royal Palace (Mari, City III), upper register: restitution, inspired by the scene of fig. 2.15, of the pattern of the King trampling his enemies. Module 2. h.: 1-1.10m. Muller 1990: extraction of pl. XXV.....................23

Figure 2.15: Restitution drawing of the impression of a seal known from different clay door-lock sealings from the Great Royal Palace (Mari, City III) inscribed with the name of Mukannishum, intendant of the palace: the King hits a standing enemy with his *harpè* while he tramples a cluster of five others collapsed to the ground. Beyer in Margueron 2004: fig. 506-2 and cf. Amiet 1960: fig. 12; Parrot 1959: 189-191. 23

Figure 2.16: Modern impression of the seal of Ana-Sin-taklâku. A lot of his sealings (especially of jars) were found in the Great Royal Palace (Mari, City III): the King, surrounded by deities and holding an *harpè* tramples an enemy. H. 2.7cm. Louvre AO 21988. Beyer in Margueron 2004: fig. 506-1; cf. Amiet 1960: fig. 13; Parrot 1959: 169-185.....................24

Figure 2.17: Iconographic and architectural restitution of paintings of room 220', south wall, of the Great Royal Palace (Mari, City III). H. 3.50m c., L. 14.75m. Margueron *et al*. 1990: fig. 11.....................24

Figure 2.18: Fragments of wall painting on coating of *juss* from the court 106 of the Great Royal Palace (Mari, City III) : presentation panel conceived by B. Muller and realized after restoration by CEPMR/CNRS (Centre d'Etudes de Peintures Murales Romaines, Soissons) under the direction of A. Barbet for the Louvre Museum. « Le Grand Palais Royal de Mari (2000-1760 a) », *Actualités du Département des Antiquités Orientales* n° 21 (4th December 2013-2nd June 2014). 25

Figure 2.19: Restitution drawing of the impression of the seal (n° 1) of Ishqi-Mari from different sealings discovered in room 11 of the pseudo-Palace (Mari, City II) : battle and banquet celebrating victory. Beyer 2007: fig. 17. Scale 2: 1.....................26

Visualizing War in the Old Babylonian Period: Drama and Canon

Figure 3.1: Victory Stele of Eannatum. From Tello. Early Dynastic period. Louvre Museum (after Forest 1996: 222). 29

Figure 3.2: Victory Stele of King Dadusha of Eshnunna. From Tell Asmar. Old Babylonian period. Baghdad Museum (after Ismail and Cavigneaux 2003: pl. 34) 31

Figure 3.3: Neo-Assyrian bas-relief. From Nineveh. North Palace, Room S. Reign of Ashurbanipal. British Museum (after Orthmann 1975: 325, pl. 247).....................32

Figure 3.4: Cylinder seal. Newell Collection. Old Babylonian period (after von der Osten 1934: pl. 14: 155) 33

Figure 3.5: Cylinder seal. Moore Collection. Old Babylonian period (after Eisen 1940: pl. 7: 60) 33

Figure 3.6: Victory Stele of Naramsin. Akkadian period. Louvre Museum (after Orthmann 1975: 196, pl. 196).....................34

Figure 3.7: Terracotta Plaque. From Kish. Old Babylonian Period. Baghdad Museum (after Moorey 1975: pl. 23a).....................35

Middle Assyrian Drama in Depicting War: a Step towards Neo-Assyrian Art

Figure 4.1: Pyxis lid from Assur (Berlin, Vorderasiatische Museum, VA7989), 13th s. BC. Source: Matthiae 1997: 32.....................37

Figure 4.2: stone Cult Pedestal of Tukulti-Ninurta I. Source: Matthiae 1997: 31-32. 38

Figure 4.3: stele from Suse (Louvre, Sb 7). Source: Matthiae 2000: 52.....................39

Figure 4.4: Hunt seals Source: Harper *et alii* 1995: 65-66, fig. 26 ; Invernizzi 1992 : n° 310. 39

Figure 4.5: Broken Obelisk of Assur-bel-kala (11th century BC), from Nineveh. Source: Matthiae 1997: 33.....................40

Figure 4.6: Old Babylonian terracotta representing the epiphany of god (Philadelphie, Penn Museum, Y.B.C. 10.035). Source: Opificius 1961: n° 399. 40

Figure 4.7: Urban settings of Kar-Tukulti-Ninurta and Dur-Sharrukin. Source: original setting. 41

"Losing One's Head". Some Hints on Procedures and Meanings of Decapitation in the Ancient Near East

Figure 5.1: Neo-Assyrian bas relief. 46

Figure 5.2: Detail of the Stele of Vultures (III mill. BC) 47

Figure 5.3: Example of paintings from Catal Höyük.....................47

Figure 5.4: Heaps of SH piled up next to valuable furnishings and weapons, Neo-Assyrian period. 48

Figure 5.5: Soldiers bringing decapitated heads. From Ebla, III mill. BC.....................49

Figure 5.6: Soldiers bringing decapitated heads. From Tell Taynat, I mill. BC.....................49

Figure 5.7: Removal of SH and their transportation to the place of "counting". Neo-Assyrian period. 50

Figure 5.8: Heads became food for birds of prey, example from Uruk glyptic. 51

Figure 5.9: Heads became food for birds of prey, example from Catal Höyük. 51

Figure 5.10: Flying vultures grabbing the heads of enemies, III mill. BC (Stele of vultures).....................52

Figure 5.11: Stele of the king Dadusha, early II mill. BC 53

Where is the Public? A New Look at the Brutality Scenes in Neo-Assyrian Royal Inscriptions and Art

Figure 6.1: Atrocities in Neo-Assyrian royal inscriptions 59

Figure 6.2: The addressees of the royal inscriptions. 61

Figure 6.3: Battle of Til-Tuba. A soldier holds Teumman's cut-off head (second register from the bottom, left side; Cat.-No 44); corpses of defeated Elamites are thrown into the River Ulai (lower half, right side; Cat.-No 45). From Barnett, Bleibtreu and Turner 1998: pl. 296. 63

Figure 6.4: Shalmaneser's Balawat gates as displayed in the British Museum (Cat.-Nos 3–7). Door reconstruction based on Schachner 2007: 24, fig. 6; depictions from Schachner 2007: plates 2, 4, 8, 10 and 13. 63

Figure 6.5: Soldiers carrying severed heads for inventory (Cat.-No 37). From Barnett, Bleibtreu and Turner 1998: pl. 210. 64

Figure 6.6: Grinding the ancestor's bones (upper register, left side; Cat.-No 40); soldiers carrying severed heads for inventory (second register from the top, right side; Cat.-No 41); a soldier holds Teumman's cut-off head (second register from the top, left side; Cat.-No 42). From Barnett, Bleibtreu and Turner 1998: pl. 288. 64

Figure 6.7: Siege of Lachish, impalement of three prisoners (Cat.-No 30). From Barnett, Bleibtreu and Turner 1998: pl. 330. 64

Figure 6.8: Flaying of two prisoners (Cat.-No 29). From Barnett, Bleibtreu and Turner 1998: pl. 338. 65

Figure 6.9: Soldiers flay prisoners while another one holds a severed head (second register from the top; Cat.-No 46); soldiers pull out the tongue of prisoners (third register from the top; Cat.-No 47). From Barnett, Bleibtreu and Turner 1998: pl. 300. 65

Figure 6.10: Zincirli Stele. Esarhaddon holds two ropes attached to rings pierced in Uš-Anaḫuru's and Abdi-Milkūti's lower lips (Cat.-No 35). From Börker-Klahn 1982: Nr. 218. 66

Figure 6.11: Sargon gouging out the eyes of a prisoner (Cat.-Nr. 13). From Botta and Flandin 1849b: pl. 118. 66

Figure 6.12: Brutality scenes in Neo-Assyrian art 67

Figure 6.13: The addressees of the iconographic sources 67

Figure 6.14: Degrees of accessibility to the palace reliefs 68

Figure 6.15: Location of the brutality scenes 69

Figure 6.16: Visibility of the brutality scenes 70

Abbreviations and General References

Abbreviations

AASyr.	*Annales archéologiques arabes syriennes. Revue d'archéologie et d'histoire* (Damas).
AASOR	*Annual of the American Schools of Oriental Research* (New Haven & Cambridge, Mass).
AfO	*Archiv für Orientforschungen* ; Beih. (Berlin & Graz).
AHw	W. von Soden, *Akkadisches Handwörterbuch* (Wiesbaden).
AJA	*American Journal of Archaeology* (Princeton & Baltimore).
Akkadica	*Akkadica. Périodique bimestriel de la Fondation Assyriologique Georges Dossin* (Bruxelles).
AMI	*Archäologische Mitteilungen aus Iran* (Berlin).
Amurru 2	J.-M. Durand & D. Charpin (éds.), *Mari, Ébla et les Hourrites : dix ans de travaux, deuxième partie. Actes du colloque international* (Paris).
AnSt.	*Anatolian Studies. Journal of the British Institute of Archaeology at Ankara* (London).
ANES	*Ancient Near Eastern Studies* (Melbourne).
AnOr	*Analecta Orientalia* (Roma).
Antiquitas	*Antiquitas. Reihe 3 : Abhandlungen zur Vor- und Frühgeschichte, zur klassischen und provinzial-römischen Archäologie* (Bonn).
Antiquity	*Antiquity. A Quarterly Review of Archaeology* (Gloucester).
AOAT	*Alter Orient und Altes Testament* (Kevelaer & Neukirchen-Vluyn & Münster).
AoF	*Altorientalische Forschungen* (Berlin).
AOS	*American Oriental Series* (New Haven).
ARM	*Archives royales de Mari* (Paris).
ARMT	*Archives royales de Mari – Textes* (Paris).
AS	*Assyriological Studies* (Chicago).
ASJ	*Acta Sumerologica* (Hiroshima).
Assur	*Monographic Journals of the Near East. Assur* (Malibu).
Athenaeum	*Athenaeum. Studi periodici di letteratura e storia dell'Antichità* (Pavia).
AulaOr	*Aula Orientalis* (Barcelona).
AUWE	*Ausgrabungen in Uruk-Warka. Endberichte* (Mainz).
BagM	*Baghdader Mitteilungen* (Berlin).
BaF	*Baghdader Forschungen* (Mainz am Rhein).
BAH	*Bibliothèque archéologique et historique*, Institut Français d'Archéologie du Proche-Orient (Paris).
BAR	British Archaeological Reports.
BASOR	*Bulletin of the American Schools of Oriental Research* (New Haven).
BBV	*Berliner Beiträge zur Vor- und Frühgeschichte* (Berlin).
BBVO	*Berliner Beiträge zum Vorder Orient* (Berlin).
Belleten	*Belleten.* Türk Tarih Kurumu (Ankara).
BiMes	*Bibliotheca Mesopotamica* (Malibu).
BIWA	Beiträge zum Inschriftenwerk Assurbanipals, Borger R., 1996 (Wiesbaden).
BPOA	*Biblioteca del próximo oriente antiguo* (Madrid).
BSAOS	*Bulletin of the School of Oriental and African Studies* (London).
CAD	*The Assyrian Dictionary of the University of Chicago* (Chicago).
CM	*Cuneiform Monographs* (Groningen & Leiden).
CMAO	*Contributi e materiali di archeologia orientale* (Roma).
CMO	*Cahier de la Maison de l'Orient* (Lyon).
CNIP	*Carsten Niebuhr Institute Publications* (Copenhagen).
CRAI	*Comptes rendus des séances de l'Académie des Inscriptions et Belles Lettres* (Paris).
CRRA	*Compte rendu de la Rencontre Assyriologique Internationale.*
Eblaitica	*Eblaitica. Essays on the Ebla Archives and Eblaite Language* (Winona Lake).
FAOS	*Freiburger Altorientalische Studien* (Fribourg).
FM	*Florilegium Marianum* (Paris).
HANEM/S	*History of the Ancient Near East/ Monographs/ Studies* (Padova).
HdO	*Handbuch der Orientalistik* (Leiden).
HSAO	*Heidelberger Studien zum Alten Orient* (Heidelberg).
HSS	*Harvard Semitic Series* (Cambridge, Mass).

Iraq	*Iraq. Journal of the British School of Archaeology in Iraq* (London).
Isimu	*Isimu. Revista sobre Oriente Próximo y Egipto en la antigüedad* (Madrid).
JANES	*Journal of the Ancient Near Eastern Society of Columbia University* (New York).
JAOS	*Journal of the American Oriental Society* (New Haven).
JCS	*Journal of Cuneiform Studies* (New Haven & Ann Arbor).
JEN	*Joint Expedition with the Iraq Museum at Nuzi* (Paris & Philadelphie).
JEOL	*Jaarbericht van het Voor-Aziatsch-Egyptisch Gezelschap* (depuis 1945 : *Genootschap*) *ExOriente Lux* (Leiden).
JESHO	*Journal of the Economic and Social History of the Orient* (Leiden).
JNES	*Journal of Near Eastern Studies* (Chicago).
Ktema	KTEMA. *Civilisations de l'Orient, de la Grèce et de Rome antiques* (Strasbourg).
LAPO	*Littératures anciennes du Proche-Orient* (Paris).
MAD	*Materials for the Assyrian Dictionary* I-IV (Chicago).
MAM	*Mission Archéologique de Mari* (Paris).
MARI	*Mari, Annales de Recherches Interdisciplinaires* (Paris).
MARV	*Mittelassyrische Rechtsurkunden und Verwaltungstexte* (Berlin).
MC	*Mesopotamian Civilizations* (Winona Lake).
MCS	*Manchester Cuneiform Studies* (Manchester).
MDOG	*Mitteilungen der Deutschen Orientgesellschaft zu Berlin* (Berlin).
MDP	*Délégation en Perse, Mémoires* (Paris).
MEE	Materiali epigrafici di Ebla (Napoli).
Mesopotamia	*Mesopotamia.* (Torino).
MHEOP	*Mesopotamian History and Environment Occasional Publications* (Louvain).
MSL	B. Landsberger *et al.*, *Materials for the Sumerian Lexikon* (Roma).
MVN	*Materiali per il vocabulario neosumerico* (Roma).
MVSum	*Materiali per il vocabolario sumerico* (Roma).
NABU	*Nouvelles Assyriologiques Brèves et Utilitaires* (Paris).
OBO	Orbis Biblicus et Orientalis ; SerAr. = Series archaeologia (Fribourg & Göttingen).
OIP	*Oriental Institute Publications* (Chicago).
OIS	*Oriental Institute Seminars* (Chicago).
OLA	*Orientalia Lovaniensia Analecta* (Louvain).
OLZ	*Orientalistische Literaturzeitung. Monatsschrift für die Wissenschaft vom ganzen Orient und seine(n) Beziehungen zu den angrenzenden Kulturkreisen; Orient und seine Beziehungen zum Kulturkreise des Mittelmeeres* (Berlin & Leipzig).
Or	*Orientalia* (Roma).
OrAnt	*Oriens Antiquus : rivista del Centro per le antichità e la storia dell'arte del Vicino Oriente* (Roma).
Orient	*Orient. The Reports of the Society for Near Eastern Studies in Japan* (Tokyo).
Paléorient	*Paléorient. Revue pluridisciplinaire de préhistoire et proto-histoire de l'Asie du Sud-Ouest* (Paris).
Philippika	*Marburger altertumskundliche Abhandlungen* (Wiesbaden).
PINHAS	*Publications de l'Institut historique et archéologique néerlandais de Stamboul* (Leiden).
PRU	*Palais royal d'Ugarit. Mission de Ras Shamra* (Paris).
RA	*Revue d'Assyriologie et d'Archéologie Orientale* (Paris).
RGTC	*Répertoire géographique des textes cunéiformes* (Wiesbaden).
RHA	*Revue Hittite et Asianique* (Paris).
RHR	*Revue de l'histoire des religions* (Paris).
REMA	*Revue des Études Militaires Anciennes* (Paris).
RIMA	*Royal Inscriptions of Mesopotamia, Assyrian Periods* (Toronto).
RIME	*Royal Inscriptions of Mesopotamia, Early Periods,* (Toronto).
RlA	*Reallexicon des Assyriologie und Vorderasiatischen Archäologie* (Berlin).
RS	*Ras Shamra* (Louvre et Damas), numéro d'inventaire.
RSO	*Ras Shamra-Ougarit* (Paris).
RTC	F. Thureau-Dangin, *Recueil de tablettes chaldéennes,* Paris, 1903.
SAACT	*State Archives of Assyria Cuneiform Texts* (Winona Lake).
SAA/B/S	*State Archives of Assyria / Bulletin/Studies* (Helsinki & Winona Lake).
SAOC	*Studies in Ancient Oriental Civilization* (Chicago).
SCCNH	*Studies on the Civilization and Culture of Nuzi and the Hurrians* (Winona Lake & Bethesda).
SEL	*Studi Epigrafici e Linguistici sul Vicino Oriente Antico* (Verona)
Semitica	*Semitica. Cahiers publiés par l'institut d'études sémitiques de l'Université de Paris* (Paris).

SMS	*Monographic Journals of the Near East. Syro-Mesopotamian Studies* (Malibu).
StOr	*Studia Orientalia* (Helsinki).
Subartu	*Subartu. European Centre for Upper Mesopotamian Studies* (Turnhout).
Sumer	*Sumer. A Journal of Archaeology (and History) in Iraq* (Bagdad).
Syria	*Syria. Revue d'art oriental et d'archéologie* (Paris).
TAVO	*Tübingen Atlas des Vorderen Orients* (Wiesbaden).
TCL	*Textes Cunéiformes du Louvre* (Paris).
TCS	*Texts from Cuneiform Sources* (Locust Valley, NY).
TIM	*Texts in the Iraq Museum* (Baghdad & Wiesbaden).
TUAT	*Texte aus der Umwelt des Alten Testaments* (Gütersloh).
UAVA	*Untersuchungen zur Assyriologie und Vorderasiatischen Archäologie*, (Berlin).
UE	*Ur Excavations. Publications of the Joint Expedition of the British Museum and of the University Museum, University of Pennsylvania, Philadelphia, to Mesopotamia* (London & Philadelphia).
UET	*Ur Excavations : Texts (*London*).*
UF	*Ugarit-Forschungen* (Kevelaer, Neukirchen-Vluyn & Münster).
Ugaritica	*Ugaritica. Mission de Ras Shamra* (Paris).
UVB	*Vorläufiger Bericht über die von der Notgemeinschaft der DeutschenWissenschaft in Uruk-Warka unternommenen Ausgrabungen* (Berlin),
VAB	*Vorderasiatische Bibliothek* (Leipzig).
VAT	Vorderasiatische Museum, Tontafeln (Berlin), numéro d'inventaire.
VS	*Vorderasiatische Schriftdenkmäler der (Königl.) Museen zu Berlin* (Berlin).
WO	*Die Welt des Orients Wissenschaftliche Beiträge zur Kunde des Morgenlandes* (Wuppertal & Göttingen).
World Arch.	*World Archaeology, Journal* (London).
WVDOG	*Wissenschaftliche Veröffentlichungen der Deutschen Orient-Gesellschaft* (Leipzig).
WZKM	*Wiener Zeitschrift für die Kunde des Morgenlandes (*Wien*).*
YBC	*Yale Babylonian Collection* (Yale University, New Haven).
ZA	*Zeitschrift für Assyriologie und verwandte Gebiete* (Lieipzig)
ZAW	*Zeitschrift für Alttestamentlichen Wissenschaft* (Berlin).
ZDPV	*Zeitschrift des deutschen Palästina-Vereins* (Wiesbaden).

References

Abrahami, P. and Battini, L. (eds) 2008. *Les armées du Proche-Orient ancien (IIIe-Ier millénaire av. J.-C.)*. BAR International Series 1855. Oxford, Archaeopress.

Andreau, J., Briant, P. and Descat, R. (eds) *Économie antique. La guerre dans les économies antiques, Entretiens d'Archéologie et d'Histoire* III. St.-Bertrand-de-Comminges.

Bahrani, Z. 2008. *Rituals of War. The Body and the Violence in Mesopotamia.* New York.

Crouch, C. L. 2009. *War and Ethics in the Ancient Near East: Military Violence in Light of Cosmology and History*, Beihefte zur Zeitschrift für alttestamentliche Wissenschaft 407. Berlin.

Dolce, R. 2014. "*Perdere la testa". Aspetti e valori della decapitazione nel Vicino Oriente Antico, Studi Archeologici 3.* Roma.

D'Onofrio, S. and Taylor, A. C. (eds) 2006. *La Guerre en Tête. Actes de la journée d'études "La guerre en tête" organisée par Collége de France-LAS-CNRS, Université de Paris X, Janvier 2003.* Paris.

Eph'Al, I. 2009. *The City Besieged. Siege and Its Manifestations in the Ancient Near East*, CHANE 36. Leiden.

Fales, F. M. 2010. *Guerre et paix en Assyrie. Religion et imperialism.* Paris.

Liverani, M. (ed) 2002. *Guerra santa e guerra giusta dal mondo antico alla prima età moderna.* Studi Storici, Rivista dell'Istituto Gramsci 43/3. Roma.

Meißner, B., Schmitt, O. and Sommer, M. (eds) *Krieg – Gesellschaft – Institutionen. Beiträge zu einer vergleichenden Kriegsgeschichte.* Berlin.

D. Nadali and J. Vidal (eds) *The Other Face of the Battle. The Impact of War on Civilians in the Ancient Near East* AOAT 413, Münster.

Porter, A. and Schwartz, G. M. (eds.) 2012. *Sacred Killing. The Archaeology of Sacrifice in the Ancient Near East.* Winona Lake, Eisenbraun

Ulanowski, K. (ed) *The Religious Aspects of War in the Ancient Near East, Greece, and Rome*, Ancient Warfare Series Volume 1, Brill

Vidal, J. (ed) *Studies on War in the Ancient Near East. Collected Essays on Military History*, AOAT 372. Münster.

Yadin, Y. 1963 *The Art of Warfare in Biblical Lands in the Light of Archaeological Study.* 2 vols. New York: McGraw-Hil

Acknowledgments

The conference and its outcomes would not have been possible without many people's help and without the financial support of several institutions. I would like to thank all of them here.

The CNRS (UMR 5133-Archéorient) and the University of Lyon provided a solid budget and gave all the means and help possible towards the success of the conference and this publication. I am also very grateful to the Ministry of Higher Education and Research, Directorate General for Research and Innovation. It generously supported the conference despite going through a period of budget cuts. Significant financial contributions were also provided by the City of Lyon and the Regional Council. My warmest thanks to all these institutions.

But a conference is above all about people. I wholeheartedly thank the colleagues who participated with active interest in it and whose patience I put to the test.

This book would not have been published without my family showing great patience, as they tolerated a very stressed week before I handed the manuscript to the editor! And finally, this book would also not have been possible without the urgent translation from French to English by Nathalie Masure and Steve Leddy, so all my gratitude and sincere appreciation to them also!

Riom, 2016-06-13

**To the People of Iraq and Syria,
for Peace and a better life.**

**And to Paolo Matthiae and Mario Liverani, who stressed the importance of historicity in the
studies of the Ancient Near East and created a wonderful school in Rome:
Deepest Thanks**

*Of all the sciences that man can and must know the main, it is the
science of life so as to do the least harm and the most good possible.*

(L. Tolstoï, Letter to Romain Rolland)

Introduction: the War and its Representations

This book brings together the main discussions that took place at an international conference on the iconology of war, held in Lyon on 4th December 2012. Its publication has been delayed for personal reasons that made it impossible to produce any earlier, and for that I would like to express my fullest apologies to the participants and to all other colleagues, especially those who expressed a real interest in the conference. I'm also of course terribly sad that the theme of the conference remains of such relevance today in Syria and Iraq. I express the hope that the war will end as soon as possible and that life can return to normal.

The idea of organising a symposium on this theme came from the discovery of the absence of synthesis on the subject in the literature regarding the ancient Near East and from the ascertainment that this theme had rarely, if ever, been explored in the context of international meetings. Several articles have covered the subject in terms of the Neo-Assyrian period, but relatively few in terms of previous periods. The problem of war is furthermore one of the subjects that interests me the most, essentially from an architectural point of view (fortifications, their active and passive use; symbolic and dissuasive values of military works; territorial occupation and control). More recently, I have also become interested in images, so I naturally came around to the idea of combining the two themes: war and how it is represented.

Of course, the images under discussion are not a faithful reproduction of reality – they cannot be regarded like photos, capturing actual events. They are firstly subject to the chosen medium, to the material and techniques employed. They also conform to a series of stylistic principles which codify and thus limit their expression (see here the article by Béatrice Muller). And finally, they cannot make abstraction of the political, ideological and symbolic reasons that determined and justified the war being pursued. As Silvana Di Paolo stresses in the third communication, war in the ancient Near East was a kind of divine ordeal: decided by the gods, war must lead to the 'goodies' conquering 'the baddies', so that the chaotic risks disappear and the cosmos can shine in its splendour. In this case, there are many images that the winners can never replicate (see here the article of Nadali), such as partial defeats and the deaths of their own soldiers. But the images also served to inform those who were not on the battlefield, including the delegations of other kingdoms. To echo Carl von Clausewitz – who was the first to stress the psychology of the military milieu – the psychological effects of warlike images can be guessed at, but probably not completely so, because Western society today has become estranged not only from 'classical' war but even

from recent memories of it. And differences of society, lifestyle, concepts, connection with the divine and with political power no longer allow a full comprehension of all the psychological and superstitious frameworks of the past. That images of war have psychological and informative effects is demonstrated by their location: the steles and reliefs on rocks typical of the Third and Second millennia BC are generally 'external' – on the outside – and can be therefore be assumed to be aimed at a broader audience, as well as at gods. So the change in the First millennium BC, when most representations of war are found to be 'internal' (in the reliefs within the palace,– see here the article by Ariel Bagg), leads us to believe that such images are intended not for a potential enemy, as during the two previous millennia, but rather for gods and for Assyrian citizens and more likely, the members of the royal court and the diplomatic corps.

While the images certainly do not provide a full and clear account of the war, neither are they fake and, being a contemporary source, at least one part of their reproduction corresponds to a real situation. The artisan/artist who made them participated in an historical, economic, social and political context, which determined certain characteristics of his work.

Thus, the images are good sources of information about specifics that otherwise would be completely unimaginable, such as military dresses, the types of weapons, the military position in combat. In this context, anything that does not correspond exactly to other source testimonials – such as weapons found in graves or description of battles – provides an additional information base toward a political and ideological explanation. Because war, with its share of dead and wounded, required an ideological basis that explained and even justified war: the will of the gods or the spread of civilization among the barbarian tribes were just ways of idealising the expansionist desires of the Mesopotamian kings. The different ways in which war was represented can provide a basis for reflection about political strategies and propaganda, and different reading levels of artistic/craft production and the goals of power. In other words, the political value of the war scenes.

In the Syro-Mesopotamian world, in fact, the war scene can only include the king. From the outset, the "typical" war scene embodied the armed king and his soldiers, with enemy soldiers depicted in defeat. It was not during the Akkadian period that this scene was established and codified: the image appears at the end of the Fourth millennium BC. It thus accompanied the establishment of a secular and political power that participated in the transformation of the village into a town. In some seals from this time – and even on a stone relief from Kish that is now in Brussels (Musées Royaux) – the armed king accompanies the assault of his soldiers on the enemy or even strikes a losing opponent in front of a building. One can say that from the late Fourth millennium BC, the king was represented not only as a pious devotee but also as a courageous warrior. This image related to the royal function of protecting people, to presenting himself as a good father, the good shepherd, the defender of his people against their enemies and against the evil powers that were always perceived to be ready to attack humans. No danger threatens the people and the city, when the king, blessed by the gods, is able to assume his duties. And from the beginning, the war scene depicting the king binds tightly with that of hunting, which is a metaphor for a warrior king. The repeated and constant conflicts of the Third millennium BC which had every city competing against each other provoked the use of a new medium for war images: the stele. The significant change here was about scale: the dimensions of steles make them imposing monuments, visible from afar, installed outdoors or in crowded places like temples; the introduction of gods to the war scene served to endorse the king's actions and the insertion of inscriptions on the monument perpetuated the memory of the king, of the city and of war. It was the Akkadian kings who mainly used warlike representations on steles and who change the scene itself: the phalange is no longer represented trampling the defeated enemy (as in the Stele of the Vultures) but rather it is the king doing so (e.g. the stele from Naram-Sin). His size largely exceeding that of other figures and his prominent position places him near the divine symbols. This is the warrior image that will be reproduced in the Second millennium BC on rocks (Darbaud-i-Gawr, Darband-i Ramqan, Sar i-Pol-i Zohab, Darband-i Sheh Han: cf. here Silvana Di Paolo), on steles (stele of Shamshi - Adad I), on seals (from Mari, Sippar, Diyala) and even on terracotta plaque (cf. Silvana Di Paolo). The last big change in war representations happens under the Neo-Assyrian kings, at both the quantitative and qualitative levels. The war (and its symbolic pendant, the royal hunt) is represented frequently in the broadest range of media, from bas-reliefs in the royal palaces to the obelisks and steles, to the glazed terracotta plaques (mostly of Esarhaddon and his campaign in Egypt), to paintings, to the bronze decorations of doors and to seals. But while hunts remain the sole property of the king, the scenes of war slip from the king to the army between the ninth and seventh centuries BC. Assurnasirpal II and to some extent Sargon II still participate actively in war, but from Sennacherib onwards, the king is only present in war scenes as a spectator, not as a warrior. This is the reason for the increase in the frequency of army representations from Assurnasirpal to Assurbanipal. The last Neo-Assyrian kings combined a meticulous description of the battles with an ever greater insistence of atrocities practised on enemies to increase the dramatic power of the representations (see here the article of Ariel Bagg).

The conference and the discussions provoked by the papers presented at it were very interesting and profitable. The article by Béatrice Muller is more theoretical and raises important questions about the war representations. For example, what is "warrior" iconography and on what basis it can be defined? Did the war scenes follow a specific directory whereby they adopted the most varied forms? Can we determine more favourable conditions for the execution of pictures of war times (e.g. the periods of great change)? To these questions Dominique Beyer adds others: were the war scenes referring to specific historical facts or were they generic representations? The ties that develop between Mari (Second millennium BC) and Nineveh (First millennium BC) show a warrior catalogue whose subjects are fairly differentiated, suggesting the existence of a specific code for the representation of war (see also here the article by B. Muller). And probably the gestures, the position of the characters, perhaps also the type of weapons were significant, although difficult to understand today. Ariel Bagg returns to the issue of the actual historical value of representations. Starting from Neo-Assyrian documentation, with particular emphasis on the "atrocities" of war, he shows the strong coherence between textual descriptions and iconographic representations. That is also the position of Rita Dolce, whose paper stresses with great sensitivity the psychological effects of images of decapitation. This act was certainly used to count dead enemies, but was also intended as a « punishment » because of the shame provoked by it, and as a real and definite destruction, an act of annihilation and alienation (because without their head or hands none of them can be recognised: this is the reason for the elimination of these two elements during the destruction of statues). The corruption of the body, particularly by decapitation, interests Silvana Di Paolo from a more conceptual point of view. What can a society accept from the representations of war? What is a "just" punishment of enemies? Who has control of the representation and thus also the memory of war? Silvana Di Paolo shows how a society arrives at establishing a "just" way to represent war, an approach justified by the socio-economic benefits and she shows how the power elites had control of the interpretation and memory of events. Davide Nadali also focuses on "silences", that is, on the elements that the images do not show and the reasons for these exclusions. And Laura Battini concentrates her study on the analysis of the multiple and complex influences in images of war that spread from Middle Assyrian to Neo-Assyrian, especially under Tukulti-Ninurta I. What is emerging from all the articles published here is the relevance of textual data in any analysis of iconological material. And this is not only true for iconology, but for all the archaeological material discovered in historical sites.

This book could not be regarded as complete if the names of at least two other participants were not mentioned. Luc Bachelot and Yves Calvet, who participated in the conference, unfortunately did not have the time to give their paper in time for publication. I would like to thank them as well as the authors who submitted their article for publication.

References

von Clausewitz, C. 2006. *Principes fondamentaux de stratégie militaire*. Paris.

Crouch, C. L. 2009. *War and Ethics in the Ancient Near East: Military Violence in Light of Cosmology and History*, Beihefte zur Zeitschrift für alttestamentliche Wissenschaft 407. Berlin.

Kaim, B. 2000. Killing and Dishonouring the Royal Statue in the Mesopotamian World. In S. Graziani (ed), *Studi sul Vicino Oriente Antico dedicati alla memoria di Luigi Cagni*, Napoli: 515-520.

Liverani, M. 1979. The Ideology of the Assyrian Empire. In M. T. Larsen (ed), *Power and Propaganda. A Symposium on Ancient Empires*, Copenhagen Studies in Assyriology 7: 297-311. Copenhagen.

Liverani, M. 1988. *Antico Oriente. Storia, economia, società*, Manuali Laterza 17. Roma-Bari, Laterza.

Liverani, M. 1996. Ancient Propaganda and Historical Criticism. In J. S. Cooper and G. M. Schwartz (eds), *The Study of the Ancient Near East in the Twenty-First Century*. The William Foxwell Albright Centennial Conference held at Johns Hopkins University in 1991: 283- 289. Winona Lake, Eisenbrauns.

Liverani, M. 2010. 'Untruthful Steles': Propaganda and Reliability in Ancient Mesopotamia. In S. C. Melville and A. L. Slotsky (eds), *Opening the Tablet Box: Near Eastern Studies in Honor of Benjamin R. Foster*, Culture and History of the Ancient Near East 42: 229-244. Leiden, Brill.

Matthiae, P. 1993. The Representation of the Natural Space from Khorsabad to Nineveh. In M. Liverani (ed), *Convegno internazionale 'La Geografia dell'Impero neoassiro', Roma 10-12 novembre 1993*.

Matthiae 1994. *Il sovrano e l'opera. Arte e poter nella Mesopotamia antica*. Roma-Bari, Laterza.

Matthiae, P. 1996. *L'arte degli Assiri. Cultura e forma del rilievo storico*. Roma.

Matthiae, P. 2015. *Distruzioni, saccheggi e rinascite. Gli attacchi al patrimonio artistico dall'antichità all'Isis*. Roma.

Marcus, M. I. 1987. Geography as Organizing Principle in the Imperial Art of Shalmaneser III. *Iraq* 49: 77-90.

May, N. N. 2010. Decapitation of Statues and Mutilation of the Image's Facial Features. In W. Horowitz *et alii* (eds), *A Woman of Valor: Jerusalem Ancient Near Eastern Studies in Honor of Joan Goodnick Westenholz*: 105-117. Madrid.

Miglus, P. A. 2003. Die Siegesstele des Königs Daduša von Ešnunna und ihre Stellung in der Kunst Mesopotamiens und der Nachbargebiete. In R. Dittmann *et alii* (eds), *Altertumswissenschaften im Dialog Festschrift für Wolfram Nagel*: 397-420. Münster.

Miglus, P. A. 2008. Kings Go into Battle. Representations of the Mesopotamian Ruler as a Warrior. In Ph. Abrahami and L. Battini (eds), *Les armées du Proche-Orient ancient (IIIe-Ier mill.av.J.-C.)*, BAR International Series 1855: 231-246. Oxford, Archeopress.

Minunno, G. 2008b. Pratiche di mutilazione dei nemici caduti nel Vicino Oriente antico. *Mesopotamia* 43: 9-29.

Nadali, D. 2001-2003. Guerra e morte: l'annullamento del nemico nella condizione di vinto. *Scienze dell'Antichità* 11: 51-70.

Nigro, L. 1997. Legittimazione e consenso: iconologia, religione e politica nelle stele di Sargon di Akkad. *CMAO* 7: 351-392.

Nigro 1998. Visual Role and Ideological Meaning of the Enemies in the Royal Akkadian Relief. In J. Prosecky (ed), *Intellectual Life of the Ancient Near East. Papers presented at the 43rd Rencontre Assyriologique Internationale, Prague, July 1-5, 1996*: 283-297. Prague.

Nylander, C. 1980. Earless in Nineveh: Who Mutilated 'Sargon's Head'? *AJA* 84: 329-333.

Reade, J. E. 1979. Narrative Composition in Assyrian Sculpture. *Baghdader Mitteilungen* 10: 52-110.

Russell, J. M. 1987. Bulls for the Palace and Order in the Empire: the Sculptural Program of Sennacherib's Court VI at Nineveh. *Art Bulletin* 69: 520-539.

Winter, I. J. 1985. After the Battle is Over: The Stele of the Vultures and the Beginning of Historical Narrative Art in the Art of the Ancient Near East. In H. L. Kessler and M. Shreve Simpson (eds), *Pictorial Narrative in Antiquity and the Middle Ages*, Studies in the History of Art 16) : 11-32. Washington.

Some Observations on the War Scenes on the Seals from Mari City II

Dominique Beyer*

A seventeen years ago, the digs that took place under the direction of J. Margueron in the sector of the monumental doorway of palace P-1 at Mari,[1]unveiled a major sigillographic find, never before seen in previous Mari-related documentation.[1] It comprised a large number of fragments of door sealings recovered in various rooms situated to the west of the central passageway from the door of this important structure of the second city of Mari (*Figure 1.1*). Among these articles were some royal seals, belonging notably to Ishqi-Mari (formerly read as Lamgi-Mari), who is well known to have devoted his statuette of a praying royal in the temple of Ishtar uncovered by André Parrot, a statuette that facilitated the very rapid identification of the city of Mari under the bleak surface of Tell Hariri.[2] One may refer to my 2007 publication for the detailed (although still provisional) analysis, of this documentation. The intention of this current paper is to re-check, correct and pin down particular data from these various cylindrical seal imprints, which are characterised by a martial iconography that is hugely rare in the context of the seals of the great metropolis of the Euphrates.

The seals of King Ishqi-Mari

The fragments of cylinder seal imprints that were found allow the reconstruction of two different versions of the same seal of the sovereign of Mari, without doubt the last before the Akkadian conquest and the destruction of most of the city's monuments. *Version a*, the most complete and the most worked[3] (*Figures 1.2-1.4*) is represented by a number of clay fragments clearly superior to *version b* (*Figures 1.5-1.10*),[4] which I still consider to be a simple inverse copy of the first, some specifics of which will be detailed here.

The two-column emblem, in its upper section, allowed the rapid identification of the sovereign's name: Ishgi (or Ishqi)-Mari, king of Mari. The composition of the image, although quite dense, allows for the splitting of the area into two parts. The lower part is thus devoted to a dynamic combat scene in which the conquering warriors send their enemies tumbling in two juxtaposed duels, and

pierce them with their spears, the naked dead becoming the target of birds of prey. On the right is engraved the logical follow-up to the fight and the victory: attached to the winner's chariot[5] – which is drawn by a horse that is stamping on the dislocated body of one loser – is another vanquished warrior, also naked, led by a victor in a thick cloak ['kaunakès'] with an axe on his shoulder.[6] On the winner's empty chariot, as in the upper section of the war scene of the famous "Ur Standard",[7] is a human head, upside-down, which had rather embarrassed me when writing my 2007 paper. I had fretted over whether this human head could have been some kind of plaything for the scorpion pictured just above it. There is certainly nothing in that, and this upside-down head motif takes on a particular importance in the context of this victory scene. We will return to it later.

So the upper section represents the ritual victory celebration. Aside from the traditional theme of the master of animals, here is a naked hero brandishing two lions, from which the link with the royal ideology seems clear – it really is the conquering king, Ishqi-Mari, who is seated, his hair in a bun and his arms brandishing many weapons. He is accompanied by an aide de camp carrying a parasol and he welcomes his cupbearer bringing the goblet and pitcher familiar from the drinking scenes of that period. It is without doubt difficult to interpret the other figures who can be seen in this pivotal area between the king and the sommelier: if in the upper section the star, the crescent moon and the few little globes could easily correspond to divine symbols, those of the warrior Ishtar, of Sin and without doubt of other astral divinities (Pleiades?), the animal figures are to some extent more surprising. The lion can simply be linked to Ishtar, not least as he carries a weapon on his back curved like a lion's head, which I took to be a prototype of the *lion scimitar*, well known in later Ishtar iconography, although also sometimes of other divinities.[8] It is the bull that takes centre stage, in

*University of Strasbourg, UMR 7044 ARCHIMEDE.

[1] Cf. Beyer 2007.
[2] Parrot 1956. For this discovery of the first Mari temple, one should consult the exhibition catalogue at the Paris Institut du Monde Arabe: Cluzan and Butterlin (eds) 2014.
[3] By studying the various imprints we were able to restore a height of 3cm for a diameter of approximately 1.8cm for *version a* of the cylinder. *Version b* is smaller: height 2.7cm, diameter approximately 1.6cm.
[4] Photographs and drawings by the author. Beyer 2007: 249-253, 254, fig. 17-18 (drawings).

[5] Here we use the term 'chariot'– even though not entirely satisfactory – as cart is generally the term reserved for a two-wheeled carriage.
[6] This motif, barely legible on the imprints, could equally be interpreted differently: I had at first taken it to be a Syrian type of fenestrated axe, but the design and the stance of the character reminds me of one of the warriors depicted on the major inlay details discovered in palace G at Elba, who in one hand is holding two chopped-up heads of vanquished opponents, and in the other hand, a stick or a spear from which hangs a piece of clothing, some of the spoils taken from the enemy. Cf. among other references Dolce 2004: 125-126, fig. 6-7.
[7] See the excellent reproductions of these various well-known documents in Aruz (ed.) 2003.
[8] Beyer 2007: 251. In terms of the precise, sensitive chronology of these documents, this element, this detail is definitive, and for now a *hapax*, which seems to me the most innovative and suggests more an

n   TH00-11 (sceau-cylindre)

o   TH00-162, 1-42 (scellements Ishgi-Mari-A)

p   TH00-151, 1-15 (scellements Ishgi-Mari-B)

q   TH00-150 (scellement d'Ish-LAGAB-da'ar-A)

r   TH00-152 (scellement Ishgi-Mari-A)

s   TH00-161 (scellement Iddin-Ashtar + Ikun-[...])

FIGURE 1.1: SCHEMATIC DIAGRAM OF THE NORTH PART OF P-1 WITH THE POSITIONS OF THE SIGILLOGRAPHIC FINDS.

an area marked out exclusively to him, which is certainly more surprising: one should simply see him in this context as the symbolic beast of the Thunderstorm god, Addu/Hadad, or that of Enlil, insofar as this latter deity is mentioned in the inscription on *version b* of the seal (cf.

infra). Finally the scorpion, which I now no longer see as playing with the human head, must logically be part of this divine group to which victory is dedicated: is it a symbol of Ishharra, as seen later on the Kassite kudurrus? Were these different divine symbols physically present in the form of statues or various objects during the victory ceremonies? One might reasonably think so.

Agade dating than Archaic Dynasty, despite the strong presence of the Sumerian traditions.

FIGURE 1.3: FRAGMENTARY IMPRINT OF *VERSION A* OF ISHQI-MARI'S SEAL.

scenes of royal victory which are further developed on bigger works, particularly on well-known Sumerian or Akkadian victory monuments. If war scenes, especially those involving chariots,[9] are well recognised above all in the field of Syrian stone carvings, there is nothing, in any Syrian-Mesopotamian sigillographic documentation, that is truly comparable. Can we, due to its exceptional nature, consider that we are in the presence of a representation of a specific victory by the king of Mari?

Before embarking upon this sensitive question, let us look closely at *version b* of the Ishqi-Mari seal (*Figures 1.5-1.10*), pausing only in front of the differences it throws up compared to *version a*. To create it, the seal-carver (*purkullu*) seems simply to have been inspired by the imprint on the clay of the first version, which led to

FIGURE 1.2: DOOR SEAL WITH IMPRINTS OF *VERSION A* OF ISHQI-MARI'S SEAL.

To sum up, on the Ishqi-Mari seal, particularly *version a*, one finds most of the iconographic details specific to

FIGURE 1.4: GRAPHIC RECONSTRUCTION OF THE IMPRINT OF *VERSION A*.

---

[9] See Bretschneider, Van Vyve and Jans 2009; Jans and Brettschneider 1998.

FIGURE 1.5: DOOR SEAL WITH FRAGMENTARY IMPRINTS OF
VERSION B OF ISHQI-MARI'S SEAL.

FIGURE 1.6: FRAGMENTARY IMPRINT OF *VERSION B*.

him inversing the general layout of the image. The main modifications are as follows:

- General simplification of the iconography that seems to be reduced, which could partly be explained by the smaller dimensions of the seal. The wear on the imprints prevents the verification of the presence of astral symbols in the upper part of the image;
- The absence of the cupbearer allowing the lengthening of the inscription which talks of – apart from the name and title of the king – the 'priestly' nature of Enlil (PA.TE.SI/^{d}en-lil), as on the statuette from the temple of Ishtar (*Figure*

1.7). One could talk at length about this, which could have consequences relating to one's understanding of the document's chronology. This question, as with others, merits further study;
- The lack also of the scorpion, doubtless for the same reason, but this absence would confirm the link between the insect and the human head on the chariot;

FIGURE 1.7: FRAGMENTARY IMPRINT: UPPER SECTION OF *VERSION B*.

FIGURE 1.8: FRAGMENTARY IMPRINT: KING ISHQI-MARI (*VERSION B*).

two documents and of their chronology. The principal anomaly was to be found in the image of a beardless sovereign, which could arouse a legitimate doubt as to the relative chronology of the two seals. *Version b* can thus become the earlier as it could have belonged to Ishqi-Mari as conqueror, but he would not have yet been king, and on the other hand the inscription could have been re-engraved. So it was up to me to verify, as far as that was possible, the truth of document b such as I had presented in the 2007 publication. Since re-examining the originals kept in the Der ez-Zor museum was unfortunately no longer possible now, there were just the series of photographs and the moulds of some of the imprints made during the dig. Even though the documents that illustrate *version b* are far fewer in number and less well preserved than those of *version a*, I was able, despite some uncertainties, to find trace of Ishqi-Mari's beard on them and thus re-establish his true royal status. A new corrected and improved drawing had to be done, therefore, as well as the publication of some unpublished pictures that remained. (*Figure 1.10*).[11]

FIGURE 1.9: GRAPHIC RECONSTRUCTION OF THE IMPRINT OF *VERSION B* (2007).

- The absence of the conquered warrior at the rear of the chariot (*Figure 1.5*);
- There is only one dead body under the fighters' feet;
- The birds of prey attacking the cadavers are missing.

As I have already highlighted in two recent articles,[10] we must credit Brettschneider, Van Vyve and Jans (2009) for having pointed out certain specifics and anomalies in the drawing published in 2007 (*Figure 1.9*). They presented interesting hypotheses on the broad interpretation of the

One still has to come back to the question of the human head, seen in both versions on the chariot and still represented as being upside-down, with this strong

[11] Let us remember here that, apart from the quality of the seals themselves, the legibility of the documents naturally depends very much on the distortion of the clay or on the presence of fingerprints or traces of calcite. The comparison between the first version of the drawing, which I certainly did a little too quickly at the site, and the new version, allows us to see that many details were corrected other than the infamous beard, which anyway remains barely legible: the royal hair-bun has been detailed, one of the fighters has got his legs back (quite simply forgotten in the first version!), the animal-handler has been retouched, the wildcats he is brandishing are no longer leopards – or at least I did not find spots on their coats, so this was doubtless some confusion arising from the tiny bits of calcite on the clay of the prints…

[10] Cf. Beyer 2012 and forthcoming.

9

FIGURE 1.10: GRAPHIC RECONSTRUCTION OF THE IMPRINT OF *VERSION B*: NEW VERSION.

simplification characteristic of the rather awkward style of the various figures (faces) on these seals. It is this upside-down representation that had until now prevented me from considering this head as a close link with the conqueror's chariot. In fact, this vital detail can be well understood if the engraver, in order to avoid any misreading of such a small document, was keen to draw, on top of the chariot, a cut-off head and not simply portray the head of a possible occupant of the chariot who one could have understood to have been living in this case. I owe it to the insightfulness of one of my colleagues in the Strasbourg team, Monique Halm, for having brought my attention to this view during a UMR 7044 meeting about the notion of *detail*.[12] One can in consequence compare this scene of the victorious Mari chariot to that which spreads out much more widely on one of the reliefs in room 33 of the south-west palace of Nineveh: there, it is the decapitated head of King Teumman, defeated by the Assurbanipal army, which is being transported in triumph on an Elamite chariot towards Assyria, brandished by the hair (in the place) by an Assyrian soldier.[13] Thanks to its large scale, in the whole series of the various episodes of the battle that this picture belongs to, to the taste in narrative detail that characterises the Nineveh sculptor, without mentioning the written legends, there is no ambiguity in the representation: it has all the hallmarks of the beaten warrior, with his completely bare cut-off head, and one is capable of naming him. In the case of our Ishqi-Mari seals, the work of a miniaturist, outside

the inscribed cartouche it is iconographic anonymity: the unfortunate rival of the king of Mari, whose sliced-off head is certainly represented on his victory chariot, even if very discreetly and simplistically, remains unknown. But if the principle of the beheading seems to come back, in terms of the iconography, to the Uruk period,[14] we would have here, it seems for the first time, the representation of a veritable victory where all these kinds of codes have already come together, taking into account the limits imposed by the document's dimensions: the victor's chariot crushing the enemies, to which is attached the vanquished fighter, pushed or watched by a representative of the victorious army, the sliced-off head of the beaten leader displayed as a trophy on the chariot.

Thus the fundamental question that presents itself is to know how far this highly stylised martial iconography, comparable to that of the great victory monuments, could be closely linked to a very particular victory by King Ishqi-Mari. This question has already been raised and can have multiple answers.[15] From my side, I remain very cautious. The mother-of-pearl encrusted panels found at Mari in the buildings of city II, always too damaged and incomplete, could doubtless hold real surprises in store for us if we could restore them completely.[16] They could reveal something run-of-the-mill, in Mari at least, but perhaps also at Ebla or Beydar, about this iconography. On the other hand, what was the iconographic theme of the

---

[12] Cf. Beyer 2012.

[13] See Watanabe 2004: 2004, fig. 7. It is worth consulting the other contributions that appear in this same source from Iraq 66: Bayrani, Bonatz, Dolce 2004. Also Watanabe 2008 and, in this volume, the contribution from Rita Dolce.

[14] Dolce (2004: 124, fig. 5) recalls the existence of the imprint of one of the cylinders at the scene of war of Eanna V of Uruk, where this type of execution of the enemy seems clearly evident.

[15] Cf. Beyer 2007: 256-258, and above all Bretschneider, Van Vyve and Jans 2009 who advocate the existence of tight links between historical facts and warrior iconography at Mari and Beydar.

[16] See in this same volume the contribution from Béatrice Muller.

FIGURE 1.11: DOOR SEAL WITH FRAGMENTARY IMPRINTS OF IDDIN-ESHTAR'S SEAL.

FIGURE 1.12: FRAGMENTARY IMPRINTS OF THE SEAL OF IDDIN-ESHTAR AND THE SEAL OF A KING IKU-X.

FIGURE 1.13: GRAPHIC RECONSTRUCTION OF THE IMPRINT OF IDDIN-ESHTAR'S SEAL.

seals of the Akkadian conquerors, from Sargon to Shar-kali-sharri? So far we only know of some similar seals. At Mari, in the field of the seals from city II, the warrior theme is not reserved for the decoration of the royal seal, because at least one document stemming from the same archaeological context as the seals of Ishqi-Mari, shows it.

11

The seal of *Shakkanakku* Iddin-Eshtar

The dig at palace P-1 has in fact yielded several imprints on door fragments of a seal of Iddin-Eshtar, holder of the role of *Shakkanakku*, that of a senior functionary, as evidenced from the archaic Dynasty, and thus well before the appearance of *Shakkanakkus* in the role of city leader (*Figures 1.11-1.13*).[17] In the five-lined cartouche that makes up his seal, he is said to be the son of a *Shakkanakku*, but reading the name is not easy.

Certainly, on the two registers superimposed on the image, one finds the traditional theme of fights between intertwined animals in which a hero intervenes, as well as the animal trainers who take up the central area so that the war scene is limited to the juxtaposition of two duels and the representation of a vanquished corpse. On would note that the method of representing these two duels and their protagonists is very close to that of the two seals of Ishqi-Mari. The lion tamer is also close to that on the royal seal, and can be thought of in terms of making an exact allusion of royal power, in the absence of any representation of the conquering king or victory celebration. Could Iddin-Eshtar thus be considered as a senior military figure in the service of Ishqi-Mari? This notion should by no means be excluded. But it is worth noting that the imprint of his seal was found on a door seal (TH.00.161), unfortunately in pieces, along with a seal carrying the name of another king, Iku-X, of which only the beginning of the lines of the cartouche are preserved. It is perhaps Ikun-Ishar, the king before last of Mari according to the Ebla texts. His seal would thus pre-date that of Ishqi-Mari, which could also explain the importance of the more traditional theme of his seal. The stratigraphic data, even if one wishes that they can one day be verified, do not seem to contradict this hypothesis, so long as the time lapse between the reigns of the two last kings of Mari are not too large.

It is not my intention, in the framework of this modest paper devoted to the martial iconography of the Mari seals, to dig further forward into such a complex case as the one concerning the date and circumstance of the destruction of city II of Mari. My intention was above all to convey some clarifications and correct certain errors made during the original presentation, doubtless done too speedily, of these new sigillographic documents, so as to prevent these errors from spreading throughout the scientific community and leading to hypotheses that would no doubt prove to be false.

References

Aruz, J. (ed), 2003. *Art of the First Cities, The Third Millennium BC from the Mediterranean to the Indus.* New York, The Metropolitan Museum of Art.

Bahrani, Z. 2004. The King's Head. *Iraq* 66: 119-120.

Beyer, D. 2007. Les sceaux de Mari au IIIe millénaire. Observations sur la documentation ancienne et les données nouvelles des villes I et II. *Akh Purattim* 1: 249-260.

Beyer, D. 2012. Le détail signifiant. Etude de cas dans l'iconographie du Proche-Orient ancien. *Ktema* 37: 255-264.

Beyer, D. forthcoming. La barbe du roi de Mari. Où quelques poils peuvent suffire à changer le cours de l'Histoire. *Mélanges Leila Badre*: 41-50.

Bonatz, D. 2004. Ashurbanipal's Headhunt: an Anthropological Perspective. *Iraq* 66: 93-101.

Bretschneider, J., Van Vyve, A.-S. and Jans, Gr. 2009. War of the Lords. The Battle of Chronology. Trying to Recognize Historical Iconography in the 3rd Millennium Glyptic Art in Seals of Ishqi-Mari and from Beydar. *Ugarit-Forschungen* 41: 5-28.

Cluzan, S. and Butterlin, P. (eds) 2014. *Voués à Ishtar.* Beirut, IFPO Press.

Dolce, R. 2004. The 'Head of the Enemy' in the Sculptures from the Palaces of Nineveh : an Example of 'Cultural Migration'? *Iraq* 66: 121-132.

Jans, Gr. and Bretschneider, J. 1998. Wagon and Chariot Representations in the Early Dynastic Glyptic, "They came to Tell Beydar with Wagon and Equid". *Subartu* IV: 155-194.

Parrot, A. 1956. *Le temple d'Ishtar. Mission archéologique de Mari I.* Paris, Geuthner.

Watanabe, Ch. E. 2004. The Continuous Style in the Narrative Schemes of Assurbanipal's Reliefs. *Iraq* 66: 103-114.

Watanabe, Ch. E. 2008. A Compositional Analysis of the Battle of Til-Tuba. In H. Kühne, R. M. Czichon and F. J. Kreppner (eds), *Proceedings of the 4th International Congress of the Archaeology of the Near East*: 601-612.Wiesbaden, Harrassowitz.

---

[17] Beyer 2007: 253-256. The restored dimensions of the seal are: height 3.1cm; diameter 1.8cm.

Elements of War Iconography at Mari

Béatrice Muller*

The[1] documentary sources provided by the metropolis of Middle Euphrates are numerous and varied, but it must be stressed at the outset that their generally incomplete character justifies the title chosen for this contribution. Then again, the diachronic panorama they offer us can bring us to foresee certain developments in the modalities of a theme that appears in Mesopotamia on the engravings from the Uruk period (Suse, Choga Mish)[1] and of which the most detailed developments can be seen on Neo-Assyrian bas-reliefs.

At Mari, the war-related images are spread over two of the three great urban periods defined by J.-Cl. Margueron.[2] City II (c. 2500-2250 BC) mainly offered inlaid mother-of-pearl from the temples of Ishtar, Ninni-zaza and Ishtarat[3] as well as the Sacred Precinct[4] and Area 4 of the pseudo-Palace,[5] to which the Ishqi-Mari seals, found in 2000 and 2001[6] and studied by D. Beyer,[7] bring an interesting counterpoint; and to these we must add a gypsum- or alabaster-engraved plaque.[8] Some works originating mainly from the Great Royal Palace (c. 2000-1761 BC) of City III have survived which, apart from the glyptic, some baked clays and two or three examples of graffiti, take us into more monumental art in the form of painted murals and one sole example of statuary.

Graphic vocabulary: components of the military apparatus[9]

In essence, shell inlays, generally interpreted as assembled on panels whose dimensions are speculative,[10] only offer the study of separate pieces: at Mari, only two deposits had preserved connected piece, each giving a pair of characters. Such an all-too-rare occurrence merits being fully explored.[11] However it does not offer complete restorations, and the contribution of comparative material from other sites – in particular the Standard of Ur – is not sufficient to provide certainty. That is why one should begin by making an inventory of iconic signs related to the theme of war from the pieces available to us.

It is also worth doing this for the Old Babylonian period in most cases: the graffiti do nothing other than yield an incomplete sketch; the little clay plaques generally only show one or two characters; the conditions surrounding the destruction of the Palace by Hammurabi prevent us from knowing what other statues included those of a warrior wearing a chin-guard; as for the painted murals, even though the crop at Mari was exceptional relative to the whole of the Near East, it was also collected in separate elements. Apart from the painting of the Investiture which, other than the pre-eminence of Ishtar, does not have a war theme, this crop of murals has come down to us in fragments and all the restorations, as plausible as they can claim to be, have their share of interpretative risk.[12]

To get beyond the strict analysis of the 'vocabulary' – in other words, the forms involving objects that evoke war – all that remains to help us fill the gaps in documentation, apart from the 'altarpiece' upon which too little material has been too briefly published,[13] is the archaic and Old Babylonian glyptic if we want to limit ourselves at first to just the Mari site.

Costumes and weapons

Costumes and weapons from City II (ED III-b)

At first glance, what generally distinguishes the warrior is the helmet (*Figure 2.1*), thought to have existed since around 3000 BC.[14] On the statuary, fixing holes may be indicative: it is thus thought to have been made in a material other than stone.[15] But on the shell inlays, certain military figures, dressed not in simple *kaunakès* – skirted or covering the left shoulder – but in a kind of studded shawl (apparently of leather) of various lengths and with their hair styled in a kind of chef's hat shape, flat and spiky, which reminds one of a magistrate's mortarboard or the cap of a clergyman.

---

* CNRS, UMR 7140–ArScAn, Paris.

[1] Amiet 1987: fig. 1 and 3.
[2] Margueron 2004: *passim*.
[3] Parrot 1956 and 1967b. Ninni-zaza is now read: Inanna-ZAZA according to Lecompte (in Cluzan and Butterlin (eds) 2014: 254).
[4] Parrot 1965, 1967-a, 1969, 1970, 1971, 1972.
[5] Not yet published: cf. Margueron 2004: 290-295. The palace, called before "Presargonic" and now "pseudo-Palace", is a temple-manufactory (cf. Margueron 2014). The iconography of the inlays from other temples are not warlike (Couturaud 2013, unpublished).
[6] Margueron (ed) 2015: 104-106, 127.
[7] Beyer 2007: 249-253; *Id.* 2012: 258-260; *Id.* in print.
[8] Parrot 1971: 269, pl. XIV-4; *Id.* 1974: 58-59, fig. 30.
[9] For detailed technical descriptions, see Gernez 2008.
[10] "Standard" of the Ishtar temple: length 170cm, height 35cm according to André Parrot's reconstruction at the Louvre Museum; length 120cm, height 61cm according to Calmeyer's reconstruction (1967).
[11] Muller 2014a, 2016 and in print.

[12] Muller 1990, 1993, 2002.
[13] Parrot 1958: 5-7, fig. 4, 5, pl. III.
[14] Deshayes 1969: 151.
[15] Cluzan 2014: 248 and 224 (n° 96).

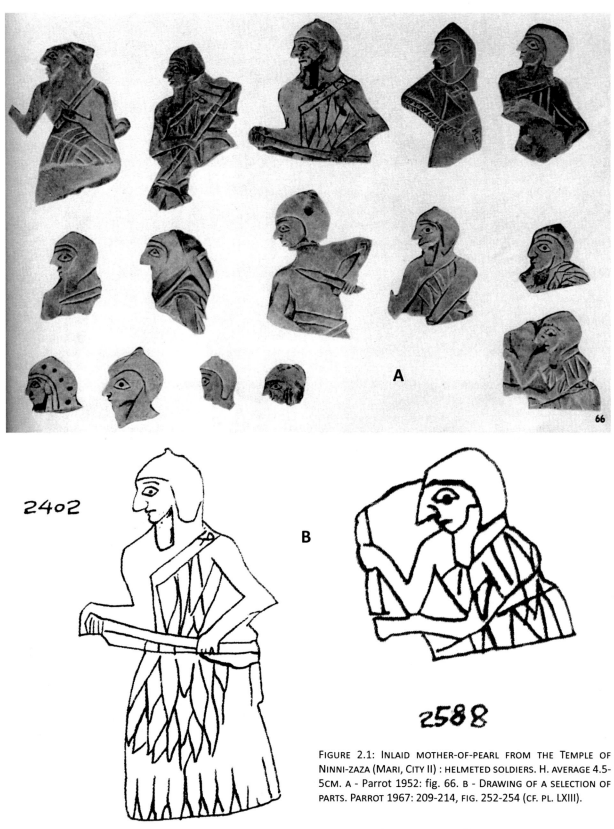

FIGURE 2.1: INLAID MOTHER-OF-PEARL FROM THE TEMPLE OF NINNI-ZAZA (MARI, CITY II) : HELMETED SOLDIERS. H. AVERAGE 4.5-5CM. A - Parrot 1952: fig. 66. B - DRAWING OF A SELECTION OF PARTS. PARROT 1967: 209-214, FIG. 252-254 (CF. PL. LXIII).

On the inlays, pole-like weapons are the most common: a lance, spear, javelin? It is the latter which supports the currently most commonly accepted identification, a weapon carried or used in different ways; it is also this that one sees in the chariot quiver; one must accept, however, that the incomplete pieces render the identification of some speculative items; the way in which the weapon is held can also give one pause for thought as to the kind of weapon. Later, there will also be the question of the axe but the inlays never show bows or shields.

14

For the latter, one must seek an alabaster plaque (*Figure 2.2*), engraved with a scene involving three characters, where a soldier, holding a pole-like weapon near its tip and dressed in a *kaunakès* wrap partly covered with a kind of longer shawl, also in a *kaunakès*, draped on his left shoulder, shelters behind a large fixed shield that he holds by curving it with one wrist, while the archer who follows him wears what seems like a stole but rigid and studded; to make the image legible, the engraver shows the archer as being left-handed, with an extraordinary effect of dropping the shoulder: he draws a composite bow, ready to unleash a barbed arrow vertically while another naked individual is in the process of falling upside-down – from high up, it seems – above the assault shield: so is this a siege scene, that would signify that the plaque is incomplete and part of a larger work? That is what is suggested by the missing elements (left hand and foot) affecting the enemy who is falling. From the shield, pictured in profile, one can get some idea of the thickness, as if it had been cut – it seems to be made of reed thatch.

Costumes and weapons from City III

Perhaps because of the risks of preservation, but in any case the documentation from the Great Royal Palace appears less rich. Certainly, the helmet can be provided with a chin-strap, which long ago established the connection between the head of the statue found on the

FIGURE 2.2: PLAQUE OF GYPSUM OR ALABASTER M. 4989-5029-5045 FROM ROOM 46 OF PSEUDO-PALACE (MARI, CITY II) : SCENE OF SIEGE (?) (FRAGMENTARY?). H. 16CM ; L. 9.8CM. PARROT 1974: FIG. 30.

A 768

B 1073

FIGURE 2.3: TERRACOTTA STAMPED PLAQUES FROM THE GREAT ROYAL PALACE (MARI, CITY III) : SOLDIER WITH A LONG WEAPON (SPEAR?) AND AN AXE. A - M. 768, ROOM 62 (near the Throne Room 65, official sector M). Parrot 1959: fig. 55 ET CF. PL. XXIX. B - M. 1073, court 87 (sector G : chambers of the staff belonging to the King's House). Parrot 1959: pl. XXIX.

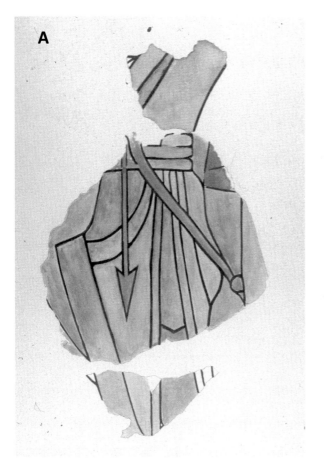

FIGURE 2.4: FRAGMENTS OF MURAL PAINTING FROM ROOM 220' (SECTOR F: ROYAL PRIVATE APARTMENTS ON THE FIRST FLOOR) OF GREAT ROYAL PALACE (MARI, CITY III). A - M. 4596 : ARCHER STANDING AT REST. H. 31CM. GOUACHE J. DEPAUW, © MAM, SLIDE A. PARROT. B - M. 4592 : END OF A BUILDING IN BRICKS BORDERED BY A FRAGMENTARY CHARACTER (POLOS AND SHOULDER) DRESSED IN A BLUE AND WHITE STRIPED GARMENT. H. 12CM.

stairway of Sacred Place 210 in the area of worship to the south-east and a detail from the painting at chapel 132.[16] The chin-strap, as evidenced by the fragment of paint that had fallen from high up in court 106,[17] certifies a jugular. Certainly, as everyone knows, the costume has changed, as already shown nearly five centuries earlier on the Naram-Sin stele: instead of a *kaunakès* there is a short tunic (*Figure 2.3*), possibly belted and with cloth drapes (*Figure 2.4*), decorated when it is of the armed king who is featured (*Figure 2.5*). But, at least from the known remains, there no long seems to be any distinction made between the soldiers (cf. *Figure 2.18*), from whom only the king stands apart.

Is the dagger specific to the king? One does not know; in any case the only clearly recognisable weapon is the bow (cf. *Figure 2.4*): originating from the room designated 220' (reception room to the king's private apartments),[18]

the handles or poles being brandished stand out well in the foreground in the brick area of the painted fragments, but their angle is insufficient to identify them. And what long weapon, tilted on the ground, is the soldier depicted on two baked clay tablets holding? This soldier also holds another, at the end of his drooping left arm, an axe of a type clearly different from those of the third millennium BC.[19] On the other hand, the gesture depicted on one of the graffiti (*Figure 2.6*) is unequivocal, as it shows a weapon for striking, too short to be a spear – probably a javelin.

Heavy equipment: harnesses

The shell inlays from ED III yielded up a certain number of equipment parts: chariot bodies, wheels, drapes, threading points, reins, quivers, all in pieces and only rarely allowing for attempts to reassemble them, very

[16] Head of statue: Margueron 2004: fig. 408; Parrot 1959: pl. VII; *Id.* 1960: fig. 336. For painting see Parrot 1958: pl. XX-2; *Id.* 1969: fig. 342.
[17] Perhaps a neck-shield is represented on the terracotta plaque M. 768 (*Figure 2.3a*).
[18] Margueron, Pierre-Muller and Renisio 1990.

[19] Inlays City II: axes with tubular sleeve collar; «the upper edge of the blade continues without interruption that of the collar» (type A) (Deshayes 1960: 155, pl. XX-1, pl.XX-2 or pl. XXI-14). Stamped reliefs, City III: «the upper end of the collet exceeds the upper edge of the blade ... « which «seems to be implanted at mid-height of the muff» (Type B) (Deshayes 1960: 170). But the very rounded shape of the cutting edge has not an exact comparison in the plates.

much like the parts of horses that break down as follows: heads, body, tails, hoofs. If the clues allow one to establish the links between the equipment parts (curved indentation at the bottom of the chariot carcass for the insertion of a wheel, reins imprinted on a threading point or a drape, bringing to mind the corresponding element) (*Figure 2.7*), none enables one to establish a syntactical relationship with the protagonists of the scenes except, at the back of the chariot body holding the Standard of Ur, the legs and bare feet of a soldier standing on the footboard (*Figure 2.8*) – which is all part of the apparatus.

In the Old Babylonian period, all this type of equipment disappears, which obviously raises questions about the extent of the documentary authenticity of these images.

Frame

While the first war images depict siege scenes wherein the town is depicted within its boundaries, where the besieged launch slingshots before being thrown from high on the walls, hit by the deadly arrows of the attackers, one must wait, it should be remembered, for

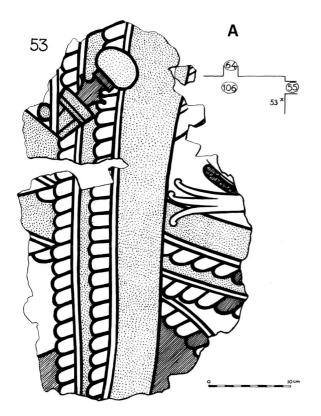

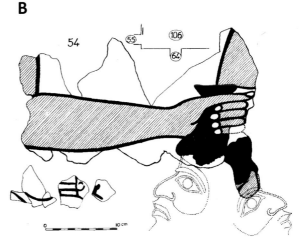

FIGURE 2.5: FRAGMENTS OF MURAL PAINTING FROM THE WEST WALL OF THE COURT 106 (OFFICIAL SECTOR M) OF THE GREAT ROYAL PALACE (MARI, CITY III) : FIGURE OF VICTORIOUS KING (MODULE 1, RESTORED H. C.1.60M). PARROT 1958: FIG. 35 AND 36. A - ELEMENTS OF GARMENT WITH RICH DRAPES HAVING SCALLOPED EDGE, A DAGGER IN A SIDE. B - FOLDED ARM, HAND GRIPPING A TUFT OF HAIR BELONGING LIKELY TO TWO INDIVIDUALS. C - PROVISIONAL RESTITUTION. MULLER 2008, NEVER PUBLISHED.

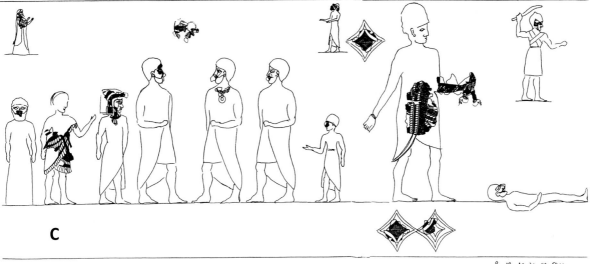

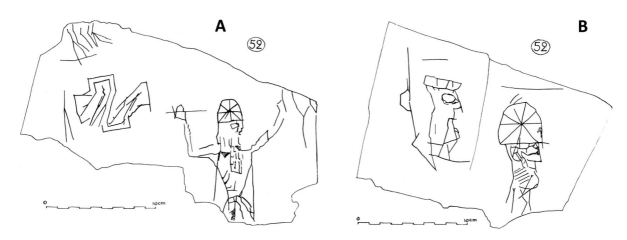

FIGURE 2.6: GRAFFITI ENGRAVED WITH A POINT ON PLASTER (*JUSS*) OF A WALL OF ROOM 52 (SECTOR H, CHAMBERS OF THE STAFF BELONGING TO THE WOMEN'S HOUSE) OF THE GREAT ROYAL PALACE (MARI, CITY III) : SOLDIERS. PARROT 1958: FIG. 13 AND 14. A - BEARDED AND HELMETED SOLDIER WHO IS ABOUT TO LAUNCH A WEAPON LIKE A DAGGER OR A SWORD RATHER THAN A FEATURE WEAPON. PRESERVED H. OF THE CHARACTER: 14CM. B - PROFILE HEADS OF TWO CHARACTERS, ONE WITH A FLAT HEADGEAR, THE OTHER WITH AN HELMET. PRESERVED H. C. 8CM AND 10CM.

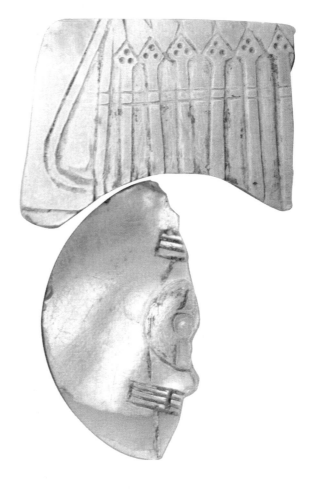

FIGURE 2.7: PIECE OF INLAID MOTHER-OF-PEARL FROM SPACE 4 OF THE PSEUDO-PALACE (MARI, CITY II) : DECK TANK SHOWING A PAIR OF ENGRAVED REINS IN ITS UPPER INDENTATION ; THE LOWER EDGE CURVED LEAVES ROOM FOR THE INSTALLATION OF A WHEEL. H. 6.8CM. NEVER PUBLISHED © MAM J.-CL. MARGUERON.

FIGURE 2.8: PIECE OF INLAID MOTHER-OF-PEARL FROM SPACE 20 (SQUARE) SOUTH OF THE TEMPLE OF ISHTAR (MARI, CITY II) AND BELONGING TO THE STANDARD: FRAGMENTARY WHEEL ASSOCIATED WITH THE BOX OF A CHARIOT ON WHOSE STEP THE LEGS OF A SOLDIER BRACE THEMSELVES. TOTAL H.: C. 7CM. © B. MULLER. LOUVRE AO 17572/19820.

limited as they may be, argue for a triumphal procession related to the taking of a city,[21] in part because of the presence of the archer as we will see later.

The figure of the vanquished enemy

No need to belabour the opposing side of the warrior dialectic: the figure of the vanquished enemy, naked, broken prisoner[22] brutally shoved along by the victorious army or torn apart by the emptiness of his defeat, stamped upon by phalanx or the royal heel, wounded or dead, or even on this knees in supplication (*Figure 2.10*), diametrically the opposite to the heavyweight military paraphernalia of leather, metal and equipment... His image barely changes across the centuries, except that in the second millennium BC he appears saved – except, perhaps, on the imprint of the seal of Ana-Sin-Taklaku (*Figure 2.16*) – the vultures ready to peck his eyes out or tear out his entrails or, in the Egyptian fashion, he is held by the hair before having his throat cut.

Elements of iconographic syntax

The reconstructions of the painted compositions have been offered, inter alia, on the basis of the proximity of the deposits, but also by comparison with contemporary iconography, in particular the glyptic.[23] The mother-of-pearl inlays, such as they are, sometimes offer clues that

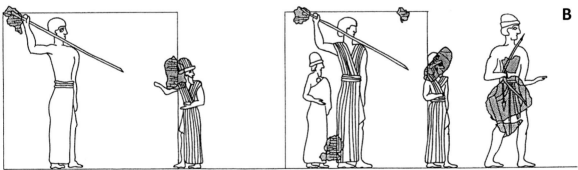

FIGURE 2.9: MINIATURE REGISTRY OF FRAGMENTARY MURAL PAINTINGS FROM ROOM 220' (SECTOR F: ROYAL PRIVATE APARTMENTS ON FIRST FLOOR) OF GREAT ROYAL PALACE (MARI, CITY III). A – Head caped with a *POLOS* BLUE AND WHITE STRIPED. (M. 4587) AT THE CORNER OF A BRICK BUILDING. H. OF THE FRAGMENT 10.9CM. © MAM, SLIDE A. PARROT. B - RESTITUTION OF REGISTER. MULLER 1990: PL. XXVIII P. 554.

the Naram-Sin stele and the neo-Assyrian bas-reliefs for a rural or urban frame to bring relief from the action. There is no such thing in our evidence from City II of Mari.[20]

As to those from City III, only the wall painting suggests buildings: five fragments from sections of wall belonging to the tiny amount collected from the great structure of room 220' (*Figure 2.9*) and a fragment of passageway (?) from the tall paintings from court 106. These traces,

enable one to associate them with certain types of figure and to place them in hierarchical order.

Soldier and prisoner

André Parrot had noticed, on the nape of most of the prisoners, two parallel engraved lines, more or less

---

[20] Nor, generally, in the iconography of the archaic Dynasties.

[21] Muller 1990: 528; Parrot 1958: fig. 21.
[22] On the inlays from Palace A at Kish they are also tied with ropes, the dignitary that pushes them holds in one hand the end of the rope coiled (cf. Calmeyer 1967: fig. 5).
[23] Muller 1990: *passim*, especially 558; Parayre 1982.

FIGURE 2.10: PIECE OF INLAID MOTHER-OF-PEARL M. 2477 FROM ROOM 13 OF THE TEMPLE OF NINNI-ZAZA (MARI, CITY II) : KNEELING PRISONER. H. 7CM. PARROT 1952: FIG. 67.

oblique, which he had first taken to be occipital folds as can sometimes be seen indeed on certain inlay parts and certain statues.[24] Now, on looking at this more closely, it turns out that the curve linking the two lines makes a finger, namely the thumb – often depicted as being exaggeratedly long – that is visible when the other fingers that are squeezing the neck of the unfortunate are hidden.[25] So the soldier's hand is depicted as a kind of stump which has just been linked to the thumb, thus a troubling syntactical relationship is created between two fragments of inlay (the arm of a soldier and the bust of a prisoner). The corollary to this is that the inlay fragments that depict this characteristic of a 'stump' do not indicate a failure or shortcoming by the craftsman, rather they automatically bring to mind the image of the prisoner. Such iconic markets would be even more valuable if the arms were not in separate pieces: that would definitively determine the types of soldiers belonging to these parades.

Now it happens by chance that the two deposits where one or even two characters were uncovered in their original collective condition give an indication on this point: the right-hand edge of the Standard (M. 474, area

20 of the temple of Ishtar) (*Figure 2.11*) and a panel fragment originating from Room 52 of the pseudo-Palace of City II, level P-1 (M. 4814) (*Figure 2.12*).[26] On then realises that two different types of soldier can hold this role: those with their hair in a flattened, pointy toque and those who are helmeted. So do the rest of their outfit and characteristics allow us to complete their identity and detect their possible hierarchy?

Clues about a military hierarchy from shell inlays

In the temples of Ishtarat and Ninni-zaza, a row of soldiers, helmeted and possibly armed, seem not to wear the leather-studded shawl but simply a *kaunakès* covering one shoulder or limited to a simple wrap. I would tend to view these soldiers as being in a lower category (cf. *Figure 2.1*), identical to the kind throwing the javelin depicted in combat on the Ur Standard chariots.[27] Certain individual pieces originating from the temple of Ishtar or Area 4 of the pseudo-Palace, also wear simple wraps of which the lower hem ends in tongue-shapes (a simplified way of representing the *kaunakès*). Given that these two sets do not seem to belong to another theme, the hypothesis of this category of ordinary soldiers can be generalised even if, stylistically and in the absence of reliable stratigraphic indications, the finds from the Ishtarat and Ninni-zaza temples would be older (ED III-a versus ED III-b).[28] But, if one believes the engraved plaque, the archer dressed in the same short kilt with tongues as his companion, differs from him by his scarf, which is not in *kaunakès*, but rigid and studded: this marks the difference of function, and probably also of de status, within the class of subordinated warriors. It should pursue investigations on codification of the suit.

The fragments connected with the pseudo-Palace (cf. *Figure 2.12*) show a helmeted soldier, dressed in a tongue-hemmed skirt with a studded strap on the left shoulder, both falling to mid-calf;[29] pushing a prisoner by the neck, he carries a spear pointed down, on the pole of which hang objects generally interpreted to be of cloth, in other words the clothes of the vanquished soldier that he has just looted. Some incomplete fragments originating from Area 4 of the pseudo-Palace suggest the same schema.[30] The outfit of the two adjoining pieces M. 471 (Ishtar, area 20) is very similar, but the incomplete weapon is most certainly different with regard to its angle and the way in which it is being carried.

---

[24] For example, statue of Shibum (cf. Margueron 2004: fig. 292 and Parrot 1967b: pl. XII).
[25] Parrot 1969: 204 and n.2.

[26] Respectively Parrot 1956: fig. 32; Parrot 1969: 205, fig. 12.
[27] With scarf *kaunakès*, unlike the fighter in the middle of figure 1a, who is shirtless.
[28] Dolce 1978.
[29] Other examples, originating from level P-2 of Area 4, show a slightly shorter strap.
[30] Muller 2016: 250-251, fig. 5b.

A

B

FIGURE 2.11: PIECES OF STANDARD FROM SPACE 20 (SQUARE) SOUTH OF THE TEMPLE OF ISHTAR (MARI, CITY II). A - BUST OF THE MILITARY DIGNITARY M. 474 *IN SITU*, YET IN CONNECTION WITH THE BACKGROUND AND BORDER, WHILE THE BOTTOM OF THE GARMENT IS VISIBLE ABOVE ON THE PLATE. PARROT 1956: DETAIL OF FIG. 32. B - RESTITUTION BY PARROT (1956: PL. LVIIA)

prisoner is confirmed by the shape of the hand projecting forward. The head-gear is not a helmet but the kind of mortarboard defined above, which could moreover only allow a single spike (M.474, cf. *Figure 2.11*) or take a taller form (Ishtar, Sacred Place 18).[31] And, as with his two cronies, the weapon is not a spear but an axe carried on the shoulder.

While awaiting the latest and more systematic studies, I propose the following distinction:

- the soldiers wearing low toque all have the shawl of studded leather that stops at the beginning of the skirt tongues; those from the temple of Ishtar are armed with an axe while those from Area 4 of the pseudo-Palace are armed with a spear.

- the leather-studded shawl of the helmeted soldiers who carry victors' spoils at the end of their downward-pointing spear falls to mid-calf like the tongued skirt. There are two constraints to this category: firstly, the association with the helmeted bust, even though seemingly similar,[32] is not proven for the fragments from Area 4; secondly, on fragment M. 4813, originating from Room 52 like the connected characters, the front segment of the shawl ends at the start of the skirt tongues; as for M. 471 (*Figure 2.13*) and M. 466,[33] they could be placed in this category by virtue of what they are wearing, but not for the weapon (which is impossible to identify) or for their stance (with a bent elbow).

Can one attempt to establish a hierarchy between these two categories that undoubtedly designate senior officers or dignitaries, and if so via which criterion? The one concerning the length of the studded shawl, the headwear or the type of weapon? As for those carrying an axe, their hairstyle perhaps hidden by characters other than soldiers;[34] would that signify a more honorific status, possibly linked to a religious role? The relative status of the weapons (*infra*)

The bust of the character linked to the fragment from the Standard, gathered up with pieces of deep shale and the red stone and white shell strips from the frame, is dressed, like its two similar companions, in a mid-calf length garment of which the shawl only falls as far as the start of the tongue-motifs; the relationship with the

---

[31] Parrot 1956: fig. 89, M. 547.
[32] Muller 2016: 249, fig. 5b.
[33] For M. 471 see Cluzan and Butterlin (eds) 2014: fig. 89h. For M. 466 see Cluzan and Butterlin (eds) 2014: fig. 89d; Muller 2016: 250-251, fig. 5.
[34] M. 4458, 4376, 4467 (pseudo-Palace, P-0 or P-1, room 24), cf. Parrot 1965: pl. XIV; M. 4817 (P-1 room 49), cf. Parrot 1969: pl. XVI-2; M. 2883 (temple of Shamash), cf. Parrot 1954: pl. XVIII-2.

A

natural grandeur (height approximately 1.6 metres), a little less in the reception room of his private apartments (room 220': height 1 metre, to 1.1 metres). In the latter, from what I could restore at the time from the intrinsic clues, the position of the remains and comparable iconography,[36] the King appears several times: a lion of a victor, stamping his enemies to the ground (*Figure 2.14, 2.15*) and standing to receive a parade of people paying tribute (*Figure 2.17*). In the great court of the official area, called Palm Tree, where the preserved paintings come above all from the southern and eastern walls, a single fragment shows him, dagger at his side, in the process of taking the heads of two enemies by their hair no doubt in order to behead them (cf. *Figure 2.5*), and the fragment of a deathly face lying nearby (*Figure 2.18*). Such incomplete remains could be difficult to interpret without the help of more explicit evidence originating from other sites.

B

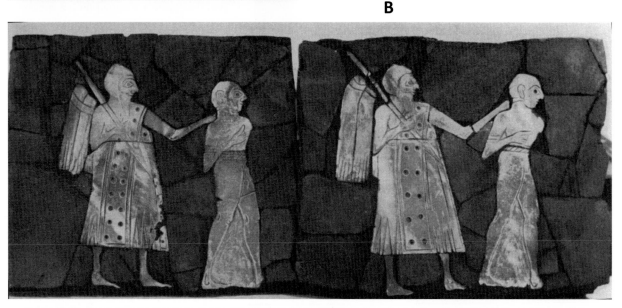

FIGURE 2.12: FRAGMENT OF THE PANEL INLAID FROM THE PASSAGE 52/49 OF THE PSEUDO-PALACE OF CITY II, LEVEL P-1: HELMETED SOLDIER PUSHING A PRISONER (M. 4785 AND M. 4793) AND WEARING CLOTHES OF THIS ONE ON THE TOP OF HIS JAVELIN WHICH IS POINTED DOWNWARD. H. OF THE CHARACTER C. 8.5CM. PARROT 1969: FIGURES 12 AND 13. A - OUTLOOK *IN SITU*. B - RESTITUTION OF A SET AS PRESENTED IN THE MUSEUM OF DAMASCUS.

would confirm the senior role of these axe-carriers, which André Parrot had predicted in conferring upon them a royal or princely rank.[35]

Warriors and the image of the victorious King in the Old Babylonian period

During the Old Babylonian period, wall painting and carving mainly represent the theme of victory, especially that of a royal. In the painting, the King acknowledges his own status by the richness of his clothing draped with decorated edges and, above all, by his superior bearing to those of the other characters. In court 106, once restored, he attains a

Furthermore, from the paintings high in court 106 (*Figure 2.19*), some depictions of warriors were of a miniature size (height approx. 60cm), impossible to place in an iconographic context and we must remember the carved clay figures referred to above (cf. *Figure 2.3*).

The axe, the javelin and the bow

These small baked clay plaques can serve to enrich the case concerning the axe, which is carried there by the basic soldier as one can also see from the same period on the Mardin[37] stele and, five to seven centuries earlier,

---

[35] Parrot 1956: 140.

[36] Muller 1990: especially 525-530 and pls. XXV, XXIX.
[37] Drawing and reference in Muller 1990: 558, fig. 2.

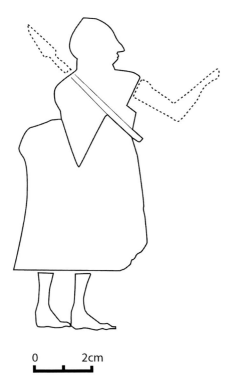

0   2cm

FIGURE 2.13: CONTOUR OF WARRIOR M. 471 (TEMPLE OF ISHTAR, STANDARD) BY COMPARISON WITH THE PREVIOUS FIGURE.

FIGURE 2.14: FRAGMENTARY MURAL PAINTING FROM ROOM 220′ (SECTOR F: ROYAL PRIVATE APARTMENTS ON THE FIRST FLOOR) OF THE GREAT ROYAL PALACE (MARI, CITY III), UPPER REGISTER: RESTITUTION, INSPIRED BY THE SCENE OF FIG. 2.15, OF THE PATTERN OF THE KING TRAMPLING HIS ENEMIES. MODULE 2. H.: 1-1.10M. MULLER 1990: EXTRACTION OF PL. XXV.

FIGURE 2.15: RESTITUTION DRAWING OF THE IMPRESSION OF A SEAL KNOWN FROM DIFFERENT CLAY DOOR-LOCK SEALINGS FROM THE GREAT ROYAL PALACE (MARI, CITY III) INSCRIBED WITH THE NAME OF MUKANNISHUM, INTENDANT OF THE PALACE: THE KING HITS A STANDING ENEMY WITH HIS *HARPÈ* WHILE HE TRAMPLES A CLUSTER OF FIVE OTHERS COLLAPSED TO THE GROUND. BEYER IN MARGUERON 2004: FIG. 506-2 AND CF. AMIET 1960: FIG. 12; PARROT 1959: 189-191.

on the lower section of the Ur Standard and from the seal of the king Ishqi-Mari (*Figure 2.20*). But the axe has acquired an honorific status: an ivory fragment, acquired in the region,[38] shows a character whose chignon headgear designates a royal figure, and he carries a sickle, a weapon normally the reserve of the gods, as well as an axe. Was this, in the high periods in any case, the preferred weapon for decapitation and, if

---

[38] Parrot 1956: 134-135, fig. 77, pl. LV.

FIGURE 2.16: MODERN IMPRESSION OF THE SEAL OF ANA-SIN-TAKLÂKU. A LOT OF HIS SEALINGS (ESPECIALLY OF JARS) WERE FOUND IN THE GREAT ROYAL PALACE (MARI, CITY III): THE KING, SURROUNDED BY DEITIES AND HOLDING AN *HARPÈ* TRAMPLES AN ENEMY. H. 2.7CM. LOUVRE AO 21988. BEYER IN MARGUERON 2004: FIG. 506-1; CF. AMIET 1960: FIG. 13; PARROT 1959: 169-185.

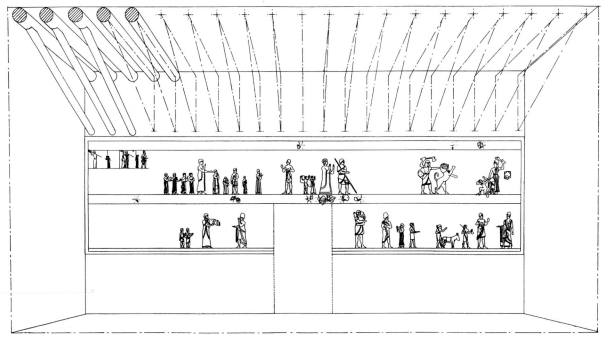

FIGURE 2.17: ICONOGRAPHIC AND ARCHITECTURAL RESTITUTION OF PAINTINGS OF ROOM 220′, SOUTH WALL, OF THE GREAT ROYAL PALACE (MARI, CITY III). H. 3.50M C., L. 14.75M. MARGUERON *ET AL.* 1990: FIG. 11.

so, can one relate it to the severed heads,[39] familiar from the paleo-Syrian marble inlays from Ebla? On the seal of Ishqi-Mari, is the head lying upside down on the war chariot behind which is the warrior with the axe not that of the enemy king?[40]

Such a prestigious status does not seem to apply to striking weapons except to symbolise the burning rays of Shamash, and it is rather at the heart of the melee where its use is depicted.

As for the bow, I mentioned earlier its absence from the inlay panels while it is highlighted on the plaque of the Archer, who is contemporary and of which the indirect

---

[39] Dolce 2014.
[40] Beyer 2012: 259.

24

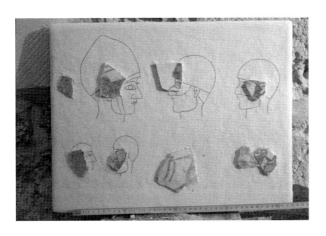

FIGURE 2.18: FRAGMENTS OF WALL PAINTING ON COATING OF *JUSS* FROM THE COURT 106 OF THE GREAT ROYAL PALACE (MARI, CITY III) : PRESENTATION PANEL CONCEIVED BY B. MULLER AND REALIZED AFTER RESTORATION BY CEPMR/CNRS (CENTRE D'ETUDES DE PEINTURES MURALES ROMAINES, SOISSONS) UNDER THE DIRECTION OF A. BARBET FOR THE LOUVRE MUSEUM. « Le Grand Palais Royal de Mari (2000-1760 a) », *ACTUALITÉS DU DÉPARTEMENT DES ANTIQUITÉS ORIENTALES* n° 21 (4th DECEMBER 2013-2ND JUNE 2014).

clues relate to the iconography of the siege of the town. Now, it is not precisely near some painting fragments from the walls that one finds the archer from room 220' (cf. *Figure 2.4*)? Is there not a kind of equivalence, a binding association, between the two motifs, the archer being the symbol of the siege? That would signify that, given the clue of a hand binding a rope on a painting fragment originating from court 106, at least one miniature scene would stand out there too relating to this theme.

Overall compositions and significance – the place of Mari in war iconography

Overall composition of the mosaic shell panels: new paths

The number of restoration proposals by the excavator himself, and then[41] of the Mari Standard, speaks volumes as to how weak the arguments were and how arguable the result. If it can be clarified, via the Ur Standard or the stele of Vultures, that the composition comprises of superimposed layers and emphasises (at least from the preserved remains) the victory parade, no element appeared to provide evidence here of the battle itself, which is one of the themes not only at Ur and Tello but also even at Mari (the seal of Ishqi-Mari) towards the end of the City II period.[42] One detail on the chariot, which has escaped all commentators, has yet to be explored:[43]

the presence of a figure (given the comparisons, doubtless a soldier) standing on the footboard. Does this not indicate that the chariot – as all the restorations show – is not stationary (the king's chariot, identified on the Ur Standard but not on the Mari Standard), receiving the march-past, but rather to the contrary, actually moving? This would then be, along with fragments M. 458 and M. 1011 (rein-guides turned towards the left and linked by P. Calmeyer with a pair of arms held out in parallel, shrewdly interpreted as those of a driver), further evidence of the depiction of the battle event; this moreover is equally unequivocal thanks to fragment M. 1103, on which the three legs suggest a hand-to-hand fight:[44] these elements too have not been sufficiently explored and markedly enrich one's understanding of the panel.

No other inlay fragment that has been found seems to provide evidence of a galloping horse, as on the Ur Standard; even the Ishqi-Mari seal includes such a detail as, in a minimal space, it manages to include most of the stereotypes found on the monumental sculpture: the enemy trampled by horses, the birds of prey molesting the dead or the wounded, the severed head and, if the infantry charge is here split into hand-to-hand combat, the armies involved are hugely diverse (spears, spike, axe). On the other hand, the unequivocal depiction of the battle is clear on panels other than the Standard (M. 4700 and M. 2481),[45] with the enemy wounded or dead.

The Ishqi-Mari seal (cf. *Figure 2.19*), if it slightly extends the triumphal march that seems to be the main subject of the war-themed inlay panels, succeeds at one level to suggest the banquet (which is, as everyone knows, the subject of the reverse side of the Ur Standard), with as the sole protagonist the majestic king, but also with the starry and animalistic presence of the gods (seen also on the reverse side of the Vulture stele), to whom the offerings of thanksgiving are indicated by the drinking jug and the goblet proffered by the servant facing the king. This theme, inseparable from that of war, could also be evinced by two fragments linked to the Mari Standard (musician? M. 400 and jug M.291).[46]

Mari and the modalities of the royal victory iconography in the Old Babylonian period

From the Akkadian empire, war chariots no longer appear in the victory iconography, as if the king alone had won, still under divine protection that is reduced to astral beings: even if he still leads his army, it is Naram-Sin alone who receives the pleas of the fugitives and tramples on the bodies of the Lullibi thrown down the steep slope of the Zagros mountains. The teeming corpses in the Ningirsu net on the Tello stele give way

41 Parrot 1953: fig. 70; archive photograph MAM 974; Parrot 1956: pl. LVI, arrangement which was following the previous presentation of the Louvre. For the new presentation, simply thematic, see: Calmeyer 1967; Cluzan and Butterlin (eds) 2014: 220-222, fig. 89-91.
42 Beyer, forthcoming.
43 Muller 2016: 248.

44 For ease of reference see Cluzan and Butterlin (eds) 2014: 220-222, fig. 89 and 91.
45 Parrot 1967a: pl. IV-3; Parrot 1953: fig. 64.
46 Parrot 1956: figs. 89 and 91.

FIGURE 2.19: RESTITUTION DRAWING OF THE IMPRESSION OF THE SEAL (N° 1) OF ISHQI-MARI FROM DIFFERENT SEALINGS DISCOVERED IN ROOM 11 OF THE PSEUDO-PALACE (MARI, CITY II) : BATTLE AND BANQUET CELEBRATING VICTORY. BEYER 2007: FIG. 17. SCALE 2: 1.

to the mass of bodies, also completely disarticulated, on the Mukannishum seal, under the king's foot, raised to prevent all resistance, as he makes ready to strike with his *harpè* (cf. *Figure 2.15*). On the imprint of the Ana-Sin-Taklaku seal (cf. *Figure 2.16*), one single body is thrown to the ground and the *harpè* hangs from the end of the arm of the deified king, depicted in a priestly stance: the struggle is over, victory is assured as is shown already by the blessing of the gods who have descended to earth in an attitude of intercession, among them being a winged Ishtar and an Ishtar Shaushga, respectively. In the two cases, the stars recall the celestial sphere. Thus the triumph, which in ED III was split into three phases (battle, victory march, thanksgiving banquet) is condense in the Old Babylonian period down to a single scene in which the kind is the central figure and he no longer retains any of the military paraphernalia of the earlier periods, just the ceremonial weapon, the *harpè*.

And let us not forget, with the small baked clay plaque from Larsa allowing sight of an Ishtar marching triumphantly above a crenulated wall and with a mass of Mari weapons where a godly head protrudes through one of the battlements,[47] that siege warfare also belongs to the divine register.

Conclusion

It goes without saying that, for the Old Babylonian period, the documentary value of the war image is reduced to zero. However, the attachment of an abutment to the outer boundary of the city of Mari, in the Amorrite period, clearly shows the use of siege machines, which will only be depicted a millennium later on Neo-Assyrian

bas-reliefs.[48] This documentary value exists in the City II era, which serves to remind one both of the depictions of solid wheels and the discovery of two wheel imprints at the level of City I of Mari,[49] and of the incontestable depiction of the composite bow on the engrave plaque. J.-Cl. Margueron compared the range of the arrows fired from this weapon with the distance between the two Mari boundary walls.[50] One could make a full list of the weapons found on the site in various contexts, but that is not within the remit of a contribution such as this one.

In City II, Mari certainly lacks examples of monumental sculpture and thus certain motifs from the period are also missing. On the other hand, the wall painting at the palace of City III makes up for the lack of attractive data on the seal iconography: like the stele at Dadusha[51] or the above-mentioned baked clay plaque from Larsa, it could well be making allusion to siege warfare, which could be considered as having been forgotten in post-fourth millennium iconography unlike the indirect hint provided by the engraved plaque of the Archer; moreover, the parade of subjected people from room 220' shows – instead of counting prisoners as in the earlier period – processions of people conquered by the Assyrians or the Persians towards the royal throne. And the gesture of being held by the hair (which comes from Egypt) instead of the trampling of the beaten enemy is perpetuated on the Recent Bronze on part of an ivory piece of furniture from Ougarit, as later, on the wall painting from Til Barsib.[52] The chronological gap is even bigger between

47 Alexander 1970.
48 Margueron 2004: 443-446.
49 Butterlin and Margueron 2006; Margueron 2004: 97; Margueron (ed) 2015: 143 and 170; Muller 2014b: 59, 67-69.
50 Margueron 2004: 140.
51 Cf. Dolce 2014: fig. 20c.
52 Parrot 1960: figs. 115, 116.

the assault shield from the Archer plaque and those on the neo-Assyrian bas-reliefs,[53] though their depiction is similar. So Mari could boast of being a major milestone in the continuity of war-themed iconography in the Syro-Mesopotamian basin.

As for the historical authenticity of all these images, the debate can be considered to be regarding the shell inlay panels. The recurrence and even the nature of the motifs and themes, plus the lack of inscriptions, all combine to prevent these from being seen to be evidence of historical facts. A slightly different question arises regarding the paintings from the Great Royal Palace: long thought to be the work of the last sovereign, Zimri-Lim, the painting of the investiture – which is only of a very secondary concern to us here – would date from far earlier, for both technical[54] and iconological[55] reasons, to one of the first Amorrite rulers, whereas, as Anton Moortgat proposed for stylistic reasons,[56] it is to Yahdun-Lim who, given architectural evolution considerations,[57] remains attributed for the paintings high up in court 106 as well as those in the king's private apartments upstairs (room 220'). Nevertheless, even if they have been transformed since ED III, the iconographic motifs generally remain of stereotypes applied to different media types: there again, given the lack of inscriptions, it is hard to think of these works as truly commemorative.

References

Alexander, R. L. 1970. Une masse d'armes à figures de l'époque du palais de Mari. *Syria* 47: 37-49.

Amiet, P. 1960. Notes sur le répertoire iconographique à l'époque du Palais. *Syria* 37: 215-232.

Amiet, P. 1987. Temple sur terrasse ou forteresse? *Revue d'Assyriologie et d'archéologie orientale* 81: 99-104.

Barnett, R. D., Bleibtreu, E. and Turner, G. 1998. *Sculptures from the Southwest Palace of Sennacherib at Nineveh*, Vol. I: text, Vol. II: plates. London, The British Museum Press.

Beyer, D. 2007. Les sceaux de Mari au IIIe millénaire, observations sur la documentation ancienne et les données nouvelles des Villes I et II. *Akh Purattim* 1: 231-260.

Beyer, D. 2012. Le détail signifiant. Etude de cas dans l'iconographie du Proche-Orient ancient. *Ktema* 37: 255-263.

Beyer, D. forthcoming. La barbe du roi de Mari où quelques poils peuvent suffire à changer le cours de l'Histoire. *Mélanges Leila Badre*: 41-50.

Butterlin, P. and Margueron, J.-Cl. 2006. Deux roues à Mari et le problème de l'invention de la roue en Mésopotamie. In P. Pétrequin, R.-M. Arbogast, A.-

M. Pétrequin, S. van Willigen and M. Bailly (eds), *Premiers chariots, premiers araires, la diffusion de la traction animale en Europe pendant les IVe et IIIe millénaires avant notre ère*, CRA monographies 29: 317-328. Paris, CNRS éditions.

Calmeyer, P. 1967. Zur Rekonstruktion der "Standarte" von Mari. In J. R. Kupper (ed), *La civilisation de Mari, XVe Rencontre Assyriologique Internationale organisée par le groupe François Thureau-Dangin (Liège, 4-8 juillet 1966)*. Bibliothèque de la Faculté de Philosophie et Lettres de l'Université de Liège, fascicule CLXXII: 161-169. Paris, Les Belles-Lettres.

Cluzan, S. 2014. La sculpture votive du temple d'Ishtar. In S. Cluzan and P. Butterlin (eds), *Voués à Ishtar. Syrie, janvier 1934, André Parrot découvre Mari*, Exposition à l'Institut du monde arabe 23 janvier-4 mai 2014: 241-252. Beyrouth, IFPO.

Couturaud, B. 2013. *Mise en scène du pouvoir au Proche-Orient au IIIe millénaire: étude iconographique du matériel d'incrustation en coquille de Mari*. Unpublished PhD thesis, University of Paris.

Deshayes, J. 1960. *Les outils de bronze de l'Indus au Danube (IVe au IIe millénaire)*. Paris.

Deshayes, J. 1969. *Les civilisations de l'Orient ancien*. Coll. Les grandes civilisation. Paris, Arthaud.

Dolce, R. 2014. *"Perdere la Testa". Aspetti e valori della decapitazione nel Vicino Oriente Antico*. Rome.

Gernez, G. 2008. *L'armement en métal au Proche et Moyen Orient : des origines à 1750 av. J.-C.* Unpublished PhD thesis, University of Paris I.

Margueron, J. 1990. La peinture de l'Investiture et l'histoire de la cour 106. In Ö. Tunca (ed), *De la Babylonie à la Syrie en passant par Mari*, Mélanges offerts à J. R. Kupper à l'occasion de son 70e anniversaire: 114-125. Liège.

Margueron, J.-Cl. 2004. *Mari, métropole de l'Euphrate, au IIIe et au début du IIe millénaire av. J.-C.* Paris, Picard/ERC.

Margueron, J.-Cl. 2014. Mari Ville II: palais ou temple-manufacture? *Actes du colloque international Mari, ni Est, ni Ouest ?, Damas 19-21 octobre 2010, Syria suppl. 2*: 265-289.

Margueron, J.-Cl. (ed) 2015. Mari, rapports préliminaires sur les 33e à 41e campagnes (1997-2004), 9 articles. *Akh Purattim* 3: 9-207.

Margueron, J., Pierre-Muller, B. and Renisio, M. 1990. Les appartements royaux du premier étage dans le palais de Zimri-Lim. *M.A.R.I.* 6: 433-452.

Moortgat, A. 1964. Die Wandgemälde im Palaste zu Mari und ihre historische Einordnung. *Baghdader Mitteilungen* 3: 68-74.

Moortgat, A. 1967. *Die Kunst des Alten Mesopotamien. Die klassische Kunst Vorderasiens*. Cologne, Verlag M. Du Mont Schauberg.

Muller, B. 1990. Une grande peinture des appartements royaux du palais de Mari (salles 219-220. *M.A.R.I.* 6: 463-558.

---

[53] For example Barnett *et al.* 1998; fig. 241a or 489a.
[54] Margueron 1990.
[55] Muller 2008, unpublished.
[56] Moortgat 1964: 72.
[57] Margueron 2004: 372-373, 439, 469-470.

Muller, B. 1993. Des peintures fragmentaires de la cour 106 du palais de Mari restaurées pour le musée du Louvre. *M.A.R.I.* 7: 355-358.

Muller, B. 2002. Hommes et dieux dans les peintures du palais de Mari. *Orient-Express* 2002/3: 82-88.

Muller, B. 2008. *Réflexions sur l'iconographie du Proche-Orient ancien - Images en resonance.* Unpublished HDR, University of Versailles Saint-Quentin-en-Yvelines (18 June 2008).

Muller, B. 2014a. Les éléments d'incrustation en coquille : situation, matériau, considérations techniques et esthétiques. In S. Cluzan and P. Butterlin (eds), *Voués à Ishtar. Syrie, janvier 1934, André Parrot découvre Mari*, Exposition à l'Institut du monde arabe 23 janvier-4 mai 2014: 285-294. Beyrouth, IFPO.

Muller, B. 2014b. La Ville I de Mari : un bilan (1933-2004). *Actes du colloque international Mari, ni Est, ni Ouest ?, Damas 19-21 octobre 2010, Syria suppl. 2*: 43-79.

Muller, B. 2016. Panneaux d'incrustation en coquille de Mari, Ville II : implication des matériaux et des techniques. In R. A. Stucky, O. Kaelin and H.-P. Mathys (eds), *Proceedings of the 9th ICAANE, Basel, 9-13 June 2014*, vol. 3: 243-255. Wiesbaden, Harrassowitz.

Muller, B. forthcoming. Iconographie mésopotamienne : images morcelées et recomposes. In *Mélanges Frances Pinnock*.

Parayre, D. 1982. Les peintures non en place du palais de Mari, nouveau regard. *M.A.R.I.* 1: 31-78.

Parrot, A. 1953. *Mari, documentation photographique de la mission archéologique de Mari.* Neuchâtel et Paris, Collection des Ides photographiques 7, Ides et Calendes.

Parrot, A. 1954. Les fouilles de Mari, neuvième campagne (automne 1953). *Syria* XXXI: 151-171.

Parrot, A. 1956. *Mission archéologique de Mari. Vol. I: Le Temple d'Ishtar.* Institut français d'archéologie de Beyrouth, BAH LXV. Paris, Librairie orientaliste Paul Geuthner.

Parrot, A. 1958 *Mission archéologique de Mari. Vol. II : Le Palais, t. 2 : Peintures murales.* Institut français d'archéologie de Beyrouth, BAH t. LXIX. Paris, Librairie orientaliste Paul Geuthner.

Parrot, A. 1959 *Mission archéologique de Mari. Vol. II : Le Palais, t. 3 : Documents et Monuments.* Institut français d'archéologie de Beyrouth, BAH t. LXX. Paris, Librairie orientaliste Paul Geuthner.

Parrot, A. 1960. *Sumer.* Coll. L'Univers des formes. Paris, Gallimard.

Parrot, A. 1965. Les fouilles de Mari, quinzième campagne (printemps 1965). *Syria* XLIV: 197-225.

Parrot, A. 1967a. Les fouilles de Mari, seizième campagne (printemps 1966). *Syria* XLII: 1-26.

Parrot, A. 1967b. *Mission archéologique de Mari. Vol. III : Les Temples d'Ishtarat et de Ninni-zaza.* Institut français d'archéologie de Beyrouth, BAH t. LXXXVI. Paris, Librairie orientaliste Paul Geuthner.

Parrot, A. 1969. Les fouilles de Mari. Dix-septième campagne (automne 1968). *Syria* XLVI: 191-208.

Parrot, A. 1970. Les fouilles de Mari. Dix-huitième campagne (automne 1969). *Syria* XLVII: 225-243.

Parrot, A. 1971. Les fouilles de Mari. Dix-neuvième campagne (automne 1971). *Syria* XLVIII: 253-270.

Parrot, A. 1972. Les fouilles de Mari. Vingtième campagne de fouilles (printemps 1972). *Syria* XLIX: 280-302.

Parrot, A. 1974. *Mari, capitale fabuleuse.* Paris, Payot.

Visualizing War in the Old Babylonian Period: Drama and Canon

Silvana Di Paolo*

The interpenetration between historiography and other forms of representation of the past (mythology), is a constant element in the Ancient Near East. On the one hand, legendary accounts are present in the evenemential history;[1] on the other hand, historical events become literary and almost legendary tradition.[2]

The interpretation of war does not deviate from this general framework.

For Mesopotamians, war was essentially a form of ethical behavior.[3] The reason for this way of thinking was that conflicts were aimed at defeating chaos, the disorder created by the human attempts to subvert the primordial order. It was also achieved through the emulation of the exploits of ancient rulers personifying a kingly ideal. This raises questions.

What, exactly, constitutes 'right war' according to the Mesopotamian system of thought? How is 'right war' recorded in visual media? What, instead, is removed?

Given the interconnectedness with politics and propaganda, war event must appear as a veritable act of 'creation' restoring the order of the world, wrongly subverted by causes that led to the war. The study of the narratives that represent traumatic events serves to rework critical thinking on war, and to reiterate the ethical responsibility of narration (*Figure 3.1*).[4] The relationship between war and representation of it presents troubled aspects. On the one hand, victories are celebrated on impressive artworks giving a powerful vision of triumphant civilizations that crystallize their cultural identity and values. On the other hand, any recording or recalling of war events also involves a genuine selection both deliberate and unintentional of what to remember or to pass over in silence. In addition to this, if defeats are deliberately omitted (for obvious reasons), victories over the enemy also are treated as events to be 'managed' in the historical sources.[5]

FIGURE 3.1: VICTORY STELE OF EANNATUM. FROM TELLO. EARLY DYNASTIC PERIOD. LOUVRE MUSEUM (AFTER FOREST 1996: 222).

Victories and Defeats: The Sedimentation of War Experiences

Military successes are, often, celebrated in the cuneiform texts. Among them, the lists of year-names refer to different aspects of royal action (building activities, the dedication of sacred furnishings in temples, the digging of canals, etc.) including the genesis and outcome of specific war episodes often unknown from other evidence (victory monuments, for instance). The year-names, usually referring to the most important event of the previous year, although on this point opinions differ,[6] usually recall the enemy's name, often removed from other kinds of texts, such as letters, mentioning the same war episodes.

The struggles between Isin and Larsa, defined by the alternating possessions of some prestigious and strategic Babylonian city-states is well known. The fifth and last year of the reign of Sin-iqisham, King of Larsa (c.1840-1836 BC)[7] had been recorded with the following formula: "Year Kazallu, the army of the land of Elam, Zambiya the King of Isin, and Babylon were smitten by the weapons"[8] which refers to a event occurred the year

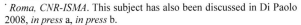

* *Roma, CNR-ISMA.* This subject has also been discussed in Di Paolo 2008, *in press* a, *in press* b.
[1] For the 'archetypal' Legend of Sargon probably built in the Neo-Assyrian period, see Lewis 1980; Westenholz 1997: 36-49.
[2] It is the case of the *Lamentation over the Destruction of Ur* belonging to the well-known genre of city-laments. On this composition, see now Samet 2014 with preceding bibliography.
[3] For some relevant comments on this aspect, see Bahrani 2008: 9-21.
[4] An important collection of essays on war in the Ancient Near East has been edited by Abrahami and Battini 2008.
[5] It remains doubtful whether, in the Ancient Near East, defeats are to

be considered examples of 'active' forgetting or rather acts simply falling out of the 'frames of attention': Assmann 2008: 97-99; Di Paolo, *in press* b.
[6] On this aspect see the comments made by Horsnell 1999: 130 with preceding bibliography. The choice of the event to be remembered in the year's name remains unsolved. A case is documented in the royal archives of Mari: Durand 1997: 157, 90 (ARMT XIII 27, 47).
[7] For absolute dates, I follow Charpin 2004: 385-391.
[8] Charpin 2004: 107 and 386; Sigrist 1990: 29.

before. Here, Sin-iqisham celebrates the military defeat of a coalition including the city-state of Isin and his king, Zambiya. Forty years later, during his 29th year of his reign (c.1794 BC) Rim-Sin, definitively conquered Isin, eliminating Larsa's only real competition in central Babylonia: this victory marked the end of Isin as an independent state.[9]

The episode of the conquest of Ur to the city of Isin by Gungunum, king of Larsa, is know only from indirect sources: Gungunum acquires the title of king of Ur in this circumstance, according to the inscriptions of the priestess of god Nanna. No year-name is dedicated to this episode by Gungunum, nor is this defeat obviously mentioned by the king of Isin.[10] A few decades later, the roles are reversed. For five years Sumu-El of Larsa lost the city of Ur to the advantage of Isin; the re-conquest of Ur during his 21st year of his reign is demonstrated by the fact that his daughter is consecrated as priestess of Nanna (this episode became the year-name of the 22nd year of Sumu-El's reign).

There is an unstable balance between the almost obsessive recalling of military victories, as the defeat of Kish by Sumu-El of Larsa during the 10th year of his reign, that is used in four successive year-formulae (from the 11th to the 14th) and a complete disappearing of war episodes in these sources.[11] The year-formulas are thought of as explicit memories of recent past events: wars become constitutive elements of a 'state' identity, reproduced in collective memory even if in a concise and simplified way. The cultural memory of a community is also built upon the balance between remembering of wars and their 'suppression'.

Within a cultural framework dominated by a single point of view, that of power elites, war memories are constructed and constantly 'commemorate' by them. This process is characterized by a rigorous activity of selection, because it promotes an orthodox reading of events and the building of a rigid image, almost paranoiac, of the world through the omission and the obscuring of some facts. What is stored for the self-preservation and posterity must survive the generations and to be kept intact. Within this process, artifacts and monuments have a special place: as objects placed at the intersection between art, history and religion, they are destined to an eternal presence in the society becoming special 'memorial spaces': cultural memory is kept continuously and periodically alive through the actions and rites performed before them and for their preservation in the future.

At the beginning of the 18th century BC, the conclusion of the peace between the king of Assyria Shamshi-Adad

and the king Dadusha of Eshnunna inaugurates a phase characterized by military cooperation that will be fruitful in the regions east of the river Tigris, from the valley of the Adhaim to the area north of Nineveh. The conquest of Qabra, known from different sources (the tablets from Mari and Tell Shemshara, as well as two inscribed stone steles),[12] occurs when this military collaboration becomes effective. Texts reveal that troops led by Ishme-Dagan together with those coming from Eshnunna, were divided in order to execute surprise attacks against the enemies and prevent their escape, thus gaining the territory as quickly as possible.

Shamshi-Adad started by attacking the countryside around Arrapha. The crossing of the Lower Zab took him to Qabra where, with Ishme-Dagan, he was victorious and conquered a series of fortified cities. In twenty days, they were able to bring the siege to Qabra, aided by the king of Mari Yasmah-Addu, and Dadusha. This event is commemorated on a stone stele, accidentally discovered in 1983 at Tell Asmar, the modern name of Eshnunna, the capital of the powerful territorial state in the Diyala basin east of Baghdad ruled by Dadusha (*Figure 3.2*). This monument is characterized by a long cuneiform inscription partnered by war scenes sculptured in low relief.[13] Originally erected in the temple of storm god (it can be deduced from the cuneiform inscription), the stele constitutes a 'memorial space', formed by a symbolic heritage embodied in text and image that serve as mnemonic triggers to initiate meanings associated with a specific war event. At the same time, it brings back the time of the mythical origins because both action and his representation reinforce the indissoluble bond between the gods and the community through his ruler and crystallizes a collective experience of the recent past.

The conquest of Qabra is, in fact, mentioned in the last year-formula of the king Dadusha,[14] when the monument was, probably, erected and dedicated in the sanctuary of Eshnunna. But it refers to the military successes of the previous year. The memory of the war is still alive.

The sequence of events seems to reproduce the steps of the military actions carried out by Ishme-Dagan. But in the project of composition of this victory stele, through the narrative of the recent past, single facts and war episodes must be 'transformed' and 'adapted' to become a shared heritage. The act of remembering war against Bunu-Eshtar involves normative aspects and includes the rules of how and what remember. To do this, the relationship between war, violence and economic prosperity (three different aspects of a winning leadership) is clearly showed through the representation of the triumph, the exhibition

[9] Sigrist 1990: 52-53.
[10] Charpin 2004: 48 and note 93.
[11] Sigrist 1990: 18-20.
[12] On the conquest of Qabra see MacGinnis (2013: 3-10) who assembled all textual data concerning this war.
[13] On this stele, see Frayne 1990: 562; Ismail and Cavigneaux 2003; Miglus 2003; Nadali 2008; Uehlinger 2008.
[14] Baqir 1949: 78, no. 13.

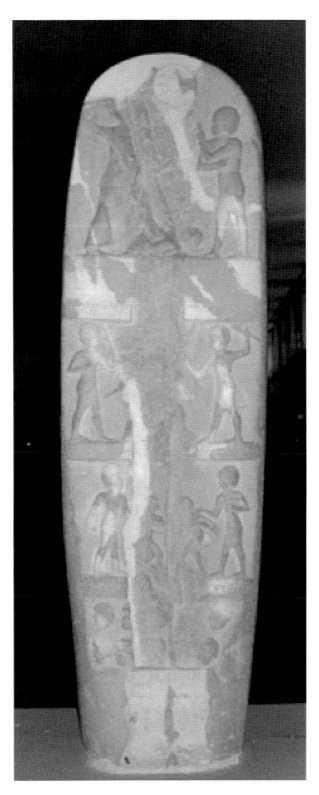

FIGURE 3.2: VICTORY STELE OF KING DADUSHA OF ESHNUNNA. FROM TELL ASMAR. OLD BABYLONIAN PERIOD. BAGHDAD MUSEUM (AFTER ISMAIL AND CAVIGNEAUX 2003: PL. 34)

certain sense, meaning and order, and overcoming the limited experience of the human life. A shared cultural memory makes use of repeated concepts that may be relevant from a social, political or ethical point of view. It is the specific experience of a community that seeks to perpetuate itself over time, trying to overcome his 'temporality'.

'Inscribing' the War on the Bodies between Aberrations and Tangible Signs

In ancient Mesopotamia, war was intended as a complex of actions and rites that took place before, during and after the conflict. In this convergence between cult and war, an important role is played by human war trophies, although the hypothesis of 'ritualized' acts of mutilation through specific cultic actions rests doubtful.

In general terms, violence and death are ritualized through the bodily dimension: whether there is an intrinsic value in the body's indivisibility as an animate whole, there is equally value in his dismembering and dispersal. The aberrations to the integrity of the physical body are related to the disruption of a individual and/ or collective identity through the theme of head and body parts removal.[15] When viewed in a wider context, episodes concerning the body's corruption may be the results of mechanisms acting to negotiate social changes through violent acts.[16]

In general terms, the practice of taking body parts of enemies within a 'war dynamic' is well known (*Figure 3.3*). But timing, methods and displaying of this cruel practice is to be understood. Within the Assyrian imperial ideology, for instance, representations of the detached heads of the enemy progressively increase in late reliefs (7th century BC) when its purpose become clearer: to register their number and display them. Therefore, circumstances and evolution of this macabre practice, as well as its display, can give rise to a number of different interpretations. Was it a stylistic choice reflecting the intention of influencing the attitudes of viewers?[17] or did it indicate a profound change in the approach to war ethics?[18]

The violence exercised against an another living being is an important component in the war ritual.[19] The performance of a libation on Te'umann's head by Ashurbanipal in order to justify the corporal destruction

---

of war trophies (the enemies' heads, including that of the defeated king, Bunu-Eshtar) and the sieges (including looting) of the cities indicated by massive turreted walls. From an authentic and specific experience, it was built a 'canonized war' through a monument requiring, in a

[15] This topic has been studied with different approaches. The human trophy-taking with particular reference to the head removal in Mesopotamian milieu has been interpreted as one of the tactics of warfare (De Backer 2009: 13-50) or as a symbolic or performative action (Bonatz 2005: 93-101; Dolce 2005: 121-132; Dolce 2006: 33-46) or both of them (De Backer 2008: 393-412). Lastly on this subjects see Dolce 2014.
[16] Hodder 2006.
[17] Nadali 2001-2003: 51-70.
[18] Crouch 2009: 54-55.
[19] Schwarz 2012: 5.

FIGURE 3.3: NEO-ASSYRIAN BAS-RELIEF. FROM NINEVEH. NORTH PALACE, ROOM S. REIGN OF ASHURBANIPAL. BRITISH MUSEUM
(AFTER ORTHMANN 1975: 325, PL. 247)

of the enemy is an emblematic case.[20] On the one hand, this episode is in conflict with the representation of human trophies left in the surrounding countryside, undermined or carried out by birds of prey. On the other hand, it shows that disfigurement acts, potentially engendering actions of divine and human revenge (above all those accomplished against another king) were carefully taken into account. Thus, the detachment of non-viable parts of body (ears, hands, feet etc.) undertakes a strong symbolic meaning as well: they are tangible and eternal signs of an individual and/or collective defeat and handicaps that forever preclude a normal life, although these disfigurements of the body of the enemy are less serious punishment acts.

A group of early Old Babylonian seals (both stone cylinders and impressions on tablets and envelopes) dating between the 19th and 17th centuries BC is characterized by a particular visual narrative supporting the legitimacy of the bodily violence and violation of the physical integrity.[21] It is a two-figures group formed by a ruling figure, identifiable by tiara and dress, and a victim, generally a seated, kneeling or lying down figure that is threatened or about to be killed. According to the visual conventions adopted, this iconic message seems to convey and evoke, with force and immediacy, emotions and behaviors of the 'audience' toward the punishment acts of the enemies.[22] Some of these artifacts come from the Diyala region, precisely from Ishchali, Tell Harmal, Tell Halawa: they are dated approximately between the 20th and the middle of the 19th century BC. The provenance of another seal impression remains unknown, although the tablet on which it has been rolled

out belong to an archive of the age of Sin-abushu, a king ruling in the Lower Diyala region. Another small group of seal impressions is coming from Sippar (almost all from Tell Abu Habbah): they can be also attributed to the early Old Babylonian period. They span a very short period of time between the reigns of Sumu-la-El and Sabium of Babylon (19th century). Among them, there is also an hematite cylinder seal: it is probably the product of Sippar workshops active at the time of Sumu-la-El.

A group of images appear on twenty cylinder seals, almost all in hematite except for a specimen in felsite belonging to the Pierpont Morgan Library Collection (*Figures 3.4-5*). Almost all of them is uncertain in dating and very scanty information concern their provenance. Only for the seal of Berlin it is possible to suggest a provenance from Sippar for the rendering of the divine kaunakès.

The act is represented as a direct and corporal assault, It channels the violent potential of an institutional figure that re-establishes the world's order against another figure, probably personifying a group who had subverted that order, The violence scene involves always only two figures, except some cases in which a third personage (an armed figure) is acting in order to block the enemy's head and permit his detachment.

On the left side there is always a ranked figure: he is often a king or ruler according to his dress and headgear, sometimes a recognizable god. On the right one a powerless man is threatened and about to be wounded or, more often, killed. They form a 'visual unity' characterized by well defined positions, gestures and acts. The performer of this action is a winner in all senses. He is erected and standing with legs slightly apart. His enemy is always 'close to the ground': lying supine or prone, often half-kneeling. As sub-human

---

[20] Bonatz 2005: 93-101.
[21] They have been described and classified (Di Paolo: *in press* a).
[22] On the persuasive power of rhetorical images and their capacity to influence beliefs, attitudes and actions of the audience, see Hill 2004: 25-40.

FIGURE 3.4: CYLINDER SEAL. NEWELL COLLECTION. OLD BABYLONIAN PERIOD (AFTER VON DER OSTEN 1934: PL. 14: 155)

FIGURE 3.5: CYLINDER SEAL. MOORE COLLECTION. OLD BABYLONIAN PERIOD (AFTER EISEN 1940: PL. 7: 60)

being, he is naked and bald shaved. Only in some cases, he seems to have a dignity: then, he is standing or in a slightly bent position, he is dressed and bearded. The corporeality is an essential component. The action is almost exclusively carried out by the figure on the left side. His main weapon, an harpé held with the right hand, minimizes the stress condition typical in hand-to-hand fighting, because immediately stop the action with the killing of the adversary. The body is also used to step up his technical supremacy and slow down the movements of the victim, immobilize him with his left arm and right leg. Thus, the aggressor easily acts against an adversary who can only suffer the blows.

Assault and killing focus on some specific body parts (eyes, hands, knees, calves, etc.).

The physical contrast is exerted in order to decentralize, to ground, neutralize the victim, also from a psychological point of view. To reach this objective, the assailant is preventing the movement of the adversary using his left foot and exercising an obstacle action on vital points of the other body: he stops the victim in his chest (where his heart is), but also to his legs (often to one of his calves) to prevent the escape. The action is not only aimed at killing and destroying the enemy (detaching his head), but also to partially attempt to his physical integrity, removing non-viable parts of body such as the hands: more often the right one, more rarely the left one. This powerful visual message is not fluctuating in an avoid space; it is inserted in a religious and, perhaps, cosmological context acquiring each time different values and meanings.

Some important variations within what looks like a canonical scheme (a kind of 'liturgical' presentation) could reveal more complex events characterized by religious, secular and magical actions, all together performed in order to neutralize the adversary. In these cases, the aggressive act could be interpreted as a 'violence ritual' or 'power ritual' performed during or after a war and always accompanied by religious ceremonies that take place inside the temples and in presence of the ruling king who is, together with a god, becomes the main personage of the scene.

The symbolic dimension of the trampling position that in this period is reserved either to gods and rulers is realized through an ideal overlapping of more figures and rules in order to incapacitate the enemy on a religious, military and magical level. Cylinder seals are a good vehicle for certain messages. It was, certainly, a particular audience, sensitive to the relationships between a secular and sanctioning violence (a necessary political tool to maintain order) and the sacred: the image of 'a power ritual' is aimed to potentiate and glorify the military actions of the kings with the divine support (a well known aspect in contemporary texts) and to prompt emotional reactions in the audience through a visual and 'didactic' rhetoric.

The Power of Symbols: the 'Canon' of Naram-Sin

Still on war rhetoric. The power ritual as a means to reinforce the idea of a perfect kingship potentiated with the divine support is constantly renewed, because information that are expressed in visual form promote the construction of mental images and produce emotions. Some war images tend to prompt emotional reactions: once the viewer's emotions are excited, they tend to override his rational faculties, resulting in a response that is unreflective and irrational.[23] So here is an important reason for conveying a concept visually: one can communicate visually with much more force and immediacy than verbal communication allows.

The king on foot, trampling on the enemy, according to a formula which goes back at least to the age of Naramsin of Akkad in the famous Victory Stele erected in the temple of Sippar in the third quarter of the 23rd century BC is again adopted in Old Babylonian period (*Figure 3.6*).[24] This image had been codified for centuries by the time of Hammurabi, as it had also been used by the kings of Ur III to celebrate their military victories, and must have still had at that period powerful political and ideological implications, since it was connected to the legendary figure of Naram-Sin. The same 'canon' is

---

[23] On the power of the rhetorical images, see Hill 2004: 25-40.
[24] Di Paolo 2008: 343-359.

FIGURE 3.6: VICTORY STELE OF NARAMSIN. AKKADIAN PERIOD.
LOUVRE MUSEUM (AFTER ORTHMANN 1975: 196, PL. 196)

Ramqan (on Lower Zab) two other similar scenes were probably sculpted: a sun and crescent are preserved in one case, a triumphant royal figure facing Ishtar is still visible in the second relief.

Four rock carvings are at Sar i-Pol-i Zohab, west of Behistun (Iran) near the Iraqi border and the Great Khorasan Road.[26] They depict astral symbols hovering over the armed king who is in a triumphal pose trampling his fallen and naked enemies and facing (in all three cases) the goddess Ištar. The most famous and complete has an inscription which certainly identifies him as 'Annubanini, king of Lullubum'. A ruler with his foot on prostrate enemies is represented at Darband-i Sheh Han (near Sarpol). This process of appropriation of Mesopotamian symbols, gestures and iconographies can be also appreciated on the rock-relief now preserved in the Israel Museum of Jerusalem and depicting Iddin-Sin, king of Shimurrum (a kingdom in the Transtigris area) and contemporary of Išbi-Erra of Isin (2019-1987 BC).[27]

Some of these rock-reliefs mark, perhaps, the extent of the military conquests of the kings of Shimurrum: new archaeological research has placed its centre near the modern village of Bitwata (further north); others have identified its heart in the Shahrizor plain, between the Lower Zab and Diyala, with the northern extremity of the area under its control around Bitwata and the southern extremity at Sar i-Pol-i Zohab.[28] A possible explanation for the adoption of Mesopotamian models for material culture could be a small-scale migration process of highly specialized Mesopotamian people (scribes, craftsmen), taking into account that at least by the end of 3rd millennium BC the Trans-Tigridian lands were actively controlled by Mesopotamian kings who were interested in securing access to the Iranian highlands, their raw materials and arable lands.

adopted in the region between the Iranian highlands and the Mesopotamian lowlands. It is well known that local kings and rulers copied the pose and the iconography of Naram-Sin from the late 3rd millennium BC on the mountainous eastern periphery of the Mesopotamian lowlands. At least nine rock carvings (many of them very badly preserved) are located along the western and eastern edges of Central Zagros within an area comprised between Sar i-Pol-i Zohab in Iran (south-east) and Bitwata in Iraq (north-west). At Bitwata (c. 70km ENE of Erbil) a fragmentary relief of the top half of a royal figure commemorates a military victory, but the lack of epigraphic evidence does not permit identification of the main figure. The rock-relief at Darband-i Gawr (50km. south-west of Sulaymaniyah), long attributed to Naram-Sin or Shulgi, depicts an unknown king (no inscription is preserved) in a triumphal pose: his foot is raised over fallen enemies and he holds a bow.[25] At Darband-i

A rather elaborate version of this traditional stereotype of the king who, like Naram-Sin stands over a group of defeated enemies appears on an extremely interesting terracotta panel from Kish dating to the 18th century (*Figure 3.7*).[29] It represent, perhaps, a serial imitation of a Victory Stele originally erected in a local temple or in another Babylonian sanctuary. Indications in this regard are supplied by the shape of the panel, tapering at the top, and by division into registers typical of steles and rather uncommon in terracotta production. In the upper frieze the king, armed with axe, passes over a heap of probably dead enemies, supine and with their arms tied over their heads.

25 Börker-Klähn 1982: 137, 139; Boese 1973: 3-15; Matthiae 2000:

53; Strommenger 1963: 83-88.
26 Börker-Klähn 1982: nos. 30-32, 34; Hrouda 1976.
27 Shaffer, Wasserman and Seidl 2003: 1-52.
28 Altaweel et alii 2012: 1-35.
29 Moorey 1975: 93, pl. 23: a.

FIGURE 3.7: TERRACOTTA PLAQUE. FROM KISH. OLD BABYLONIAN
PERIOD. BAGHDAD MUSEUM (AFTER MOOREY 1975: PL. 23A)

In the lower register, however, appear three prisoners
who are naked, seated and chained. The adoption of this
'canon', namely of the king passing over the corpses,
axe held in the right hand and the corresponding arm
outstretched or bent at the waist, can be explained either
as a form of reiteration of a figurative scheme had become
'classic', or more simply as the tendency to copying in
other materials the ancient artworks still preserved inside
Mesopotamian temples.

This 'canon' represents a rhetorical response, that is a
process of 'accrual' in which past experiences merge to
construct a meaning.[30] Design and rhythm of the figures
provide a basis for the viewers to infer the creation of
images, emotions, and ideas. This module seems to give
adequate or appropriate visual expression to the feelings
or attitudes to be conveyed.

Taking into account that war for Mesopotamians was a
form of civilized behavior, its representation in art was
intended as a powerful strengthening of sense of identity,
and not only as the destruction of enemy's identity. Thus,
given the inextricable link between art and propaganda,
it is obvious that representations of war also reflected the
idea of the world.

References

Abrahami, P. and Battini, L. (eds), 2008. *Les armées du
Proche-Orient ancien (IIIe-Ier millénaire av. J.-C.)*.
BAR International Series 1855. Oxford, Archaeopress.

Altaweel, M. *et alii* 2012. New Investigations in the
Environment, History, and Archaeology of the Iraqi
Hilly Flanks: Shahrizor Survey Project 2009-2011.
Iraq 74: 1-35.

Assante, J. 2002. Style and Replication in 'Old
Babylonian' Terracotta Plaques: Strategies for
Entrapping the Power of Images. In O. Loretz, K.
Metzler and H. P. Schaudig (eds), *Ex Mesopotamia
et Syria Lux. Festschrift für Manfried Dietrich
zu seinem 65. Geburstag*, Alter Orient und Altes
Testament 281: 1-29. Münster.

Assmann, A. 2008. Canon and Archive. In A. Erll and
A. Nünning (eds), *Cultural Memory Studies. An
International and Interdisciplinary Handbook*: 97-
107. Berlin-New York.

Bahrani, Z. 2008. An Archaeology of Violence. In
Ead., *Rituals of War. The Body and the Violence in
Mesopotamia*: 9-21. New York.

Baqir, T. 1949. Date Formulae and Date Lists from Tell
Harmal. *Sumer* 5: 34-86.

Boese, J. 1973. Zur stilistischen und historischen
Anordnung des Felsreliefs von Darband-i Gawr,
Studia Iranica 2: 3-15.

Bonatz, D. 2005. Ashurbanipal's Headhunt: An
Anthropological Perspective. In D. Collon and A.
George (eds), *Nineveh. Papers of the 49th Rencontre
Assyriologique Internationale = Iraq* 66: 93-101.

Börker-Klähn, J. 1982. *Altvorderasiatiche Bildstelen und
vergleichbare Felsreliefs*, BaF 4. Mainz am Rhein.

Charpin, D. 2004. Histoire politique du Proche-Orient
amorite (2002-1595). In D. Charpin, D.O. Edzard and
M. Stol (eds), *Mesopotamien. Die altbabylonische
Zeit*, OBO 160/4: 25-480. Göttingen-Fribourg.

Crouch, C. L. 2009. *War and Ethics in the Ancient Near
East: Military Violence in Light of Cosmology and
History*, Beihefte zur Zeitschrift für alttestamentliche
Wissenschaft 407. Berlin.

De Backer, F. 2008. Fragmentation of the Enemy in the
Ancient Near East during the Neo-Assyrian Period. In A.
Michaels (ed), *Ritual Dynamics, Usurpation, Ritual*. Vol.
III: State, Power and Violence: 393-412. Wiesbaden.

De Backer, F. 2009. Cruelty and Military Refinements.
Res Antiquae 6: 13-50.

Di Paolo, S. 2008. Some Observations on the Defeated
in the Art of the Age of Hammurapi of Babylon (with

---

[30] On this aspect, see Assante 2002: 1-29.

Allusions, Topoi and Narrative References). In H. Kühne *et alii* (eds), *Proceedings of 4th International Congress of the Archaeology of the Ancient Near East (ICAANE), Berlin, 29 March-3 April 2004, Freie Universität Berlin*: 343-359. Wiesbaden.

Di Paolo, S. *in press* a. Bodily Violence in Early Old Babylonian Glyptics: a Performative Act?. In M. D'Andrea *et alii* (eds), *Pearls of the Past. Studies in Honour of Frances Pinnock*, AOAT. Münster.

Di Paolo, S. *in press* b. War Remembrance Narrative: Negotiation of Memory and Oblivion in Mesopotamian Art. In D. Nadali (ed), *Envisioning the Past Through Memories. Proceedings of the Conference Held in Rome, University 'Sapienza', November 25-26, 2013*. London.

Dolce, R. 2006. Têtes en guerre. In S. D'Onofrio and A. C. Taylor (eds), *La Guerre en Tête. Actes de la journée d'études "La guerre en tête" organisée par Collége de France-LAS-CNRS, Université de Paris X, Janvier 2003*: 33-46. Paris.

Dolce, R. 2014. *"Perdere la testa". Aspetti e valori della decapitazione nel Vicino Oriente Antico*, Studi Archeologici 3. Roma.

Eisen, G. A. 1940. *Ancient Oriental Cylinder and Other Seals with a Description of the Collection of Mrs. William H. Moore*, OIP 47. Chicago.

Forest, J.-D. 1996. *Mesopotamia. L'invenzione dello stato VII-III millennio*. Milano.

Frayne, D. R. 1990. *Old Babylonian Period (2003-1595 BC)*, RIME 4. Toronto-Buffalo.

Hill, C. A. 2004. The Psychology of Rhetorical Images. In Id. and M. Helmers (eds), *Defining Visual Rhetorics*: 25-40. Mahwah.

Hodder, I. 2006. *The Leopard's Tale. Revealing the Mysteries of Turkey's Ancient Town*. London.

Hrouda, B. 1976. *Sarpol-I Zohab. Die Felsreliefs I-IV*, Iranische Denkmäler 7 II C. Berlin.

Ismail, B. K. and Cavigneaux, A. 2003. Dādušas Siegesstele IM 95200 aus Ešnunna. Die Inschrift. *Baghdader Mitteilungen* 34: 129-156.

Lewis, B. 1980. *The Sargon Legend: A Study of the Akkadian Text and the Tale of the Hero Who Was Exposed at Birth*, ASOR Dissertation Series 4. Cambridge (MA).

MacGinnis, J. 2013. Qabra in the Cuneiform Sources. *Subartu* 6-7: 3-10.

Matthiae, P. 2000. *La storia dell'arte dell'Oriente antico. Gli stati territoriali, 2100-1600 a.C.* Milano.

Miglus, P. A. 2003. Die Siegesstele des Königs Dāduša von Ešnunna und ihre Stellung in der Kunst Mesopotamiens und der Nachbargebiete. In R. Dittmann, C. Eder and B. Jacobs (eds), *Altertumswissenschaften im Dialog. Festschirft für Wolfram Nagel zur Vollendung seines 80.Lebensjahres*, AOAT 306: 397-420. Münster.

Moorey, P. R. S. 1975. The Terracotta Plaques fom Kiš and Hursagkalama, c. 1850 to 1650 BC. *Iraq* 37: 79-99.

Nadali, D. 2001-3. Guerra e morte: l'annullamento del nemico nella condizione del vinto. *Scienze dell'Antichità* 11: 51-70.

Nadali, D. 2008. La stele di Daduša come documento storico dell'età paleobabilonese. Immagini e iscrizione a confronto. *Vicino Oriente* 14: 129-146.

Orthmann, W. 1975. *Der Alte Orient, Propyläen Kunstgeschichte* 14. Bonn.

von der Osten, H. H. 1934. *Ancient Oriental Seals in the Collection of Mr. Edward T. Newell*, OIP 22. Chicago.

Samet, N. 2014. *The Lamentation over the Destruction of Ur*, Mesopotamian Civilizations 18. Winona Lake.

Schwartz, G. M. 2012. Archaeology and Sacrifice. In A. Porter and G. M. Schwartz (eds), *Sacred Killing. The Archaeology of Sacrifice in the Ancient Near East*: 1-32. Winona Lake, Eisenbraun.

Shaffer, A., Wasserman, N. and Seidl, U. 2003. Iddi(n)-Sin, King of Simurrum: A New Rock-Relief Inscription and a Reverential Seal, *Zeitschrift für Assyriologie* 93: 1-52.

Strommenger, E. 1963. Das Felsreliefs von Darband i-Gawr, *Baghdader Mitteilungen* 2: 83-88.

Uehlinger, Ch. 2008. Gott oder König? Bild and Text auf der altbabylonischen Siegesstele des Königs Dāduša von Ešnunna. In M. Bauks, K. Liess and P. Riede (eds), *Was ist der Mensch, dass du seiner gedenkst? (Psalm 8,6). Aspekte einer theologischen Anthropologie*: 515-536. Neukirchen-Vluyn.

Westenholz, J. G. 1997. *Legends of the Kings of Akkade*. Winona Lake, Eisenbraun.

Middle Assyrian Drama in Depicting War:
a Step towards Neo-Assyrian Art

Laura Battini*

One often forgets how much the Neo-Assyrian period is indebted to the one that preceded it. That is partly because in historical reconstructions one tends to attribute the best inventions to the state that is politically the strongest in a given period.[1] But it is also because the abruptness with which the Late Bronze Age ended has hidden many of the links between the Late Bronze Age and the Iron Age.[2] And yet, many of what are today considered as new findings from the first millennium BC – when the military might of Assyria dominated the whole of the Near East – have their roots in the immediately preceding centuries.[3] Several examples from architecture, townscapes and iconography prove this, and it equally appears to be clear from the depictions of war. In the introduction I mentioned that the great changes in Mesopotamian depictions of war can be seen in the Akkadian period (end of the third millennium BC) and then in the Neo-Assyrian period (first millennium BC). This is true and moreover, it also proves how much the Neo-Assyrian kings were fascinated by the Akkadian dynasty.[4] But the Neo-Assyrian transformations are also hinted at in the Middle Assyrian achievements. The analysis which follows, while establishing a catalogue on the theme of war from this period, offers to demonstrate this point.

The grammar of Middle Assyrian depictions of war

There is only a limited catalogue of Middle Assyrian images depicting war – a relief from an altar, the lid from a pyxis in dark marble, an obelisk (the Broken Obelisk),

and some cylinder seals. Apart from the Cult Pedestal found in Assur and the cylinder seals, the three other pieces of evidence are broken, so it is impossible to have a clear image of the links between the war scene and other possible scenes, and thus also impossible to attain a full understanding.[5]

Unlike the altar and the obelisk, neither the pyxis lid nor the seals have any inscriptions on the parts that survive, but they have been dated on the basis of their style, one to the 13th century BC and the others to the 12th century BC. Thus, using the Middle Assyrian evidence relating to war in chronological order, first we get the pyxis, then the altar (1244-1207 BC), and then the seals (12th century BC) and we finish with the Broken Obelisk (Assur-bel-kala, c. 1073-1056 BC).

The pyxis lid (*Figure 4.1*), today kept at Berlin's Vorderasiatisches Museum under number VA7989, is small, its diameter no greater than 12cm.[6] The figurative area is divided into two superimposed elements, most probably of the same size. The figures of three enemies remain preserved in the upper section, two of them dead – as shown by the position of the bodies in the process of falling, with limbs and head flailing, which precedes and accompanies death. The third man, one knee on the ground, the other bent, his head held upside down and back by an opponent's hand, is being kicked by one of

FIGURE 4.1: PYXIS LID FROM ASSUR (BERLIN, VORDERASIATISCHE MUSEUM, VA7989), 13TH S. BC. SOURCE: MATTHIAE 1997: 32.

---

*CNRS, UMR 5133- Archéorient.

[1] According to the theory of the Centre and the periphery: the centre is innovative while the periphery remains conservative (for history of this theory, from its economic origin to the application in archaeology and history, its use, its evolution: Champion 1995). See also Rowlands, Larsen and Kristiansen 1987; Liverani 1987. This model begins to be questioned (for example, Stein 1999, but deeply criticized by Forest 2001).
More and more studies recognize the Neo-Assyrian debt to Middle Assyrian: Artzi 1997, Cancik-Kirschbaum 1997 and 2003; Liverani 1984; Liverani 1988: 588-596; Liverani 2004.

[2] For example (but the bibliography is very rich on this topic) Ward and Sharp Joukowsky (eds) 1992. Drew 1993; Liverani 1987; Masetti-Rouault and Roualt forthcoming.

[3] One could more simply say that the Bronze Age saw many of the first millennium developments. However in doing so, one is emphasising Neo-Assyrian achievements. The approach used here, instead, allows us to bracket the Bronze and Iron Ages together, which is more prudent.

For the studies recognizing the Neo-Assyrian debt to Middle Assyrian, see footnote 1.

[4] This fascination has been more widely recognised by historians than by archaeologists and art historians. One notable exception is Matthiae (1989a, 1996).

[5] Cf. Matthiae 1969, 1989a, 1992, 2003 and 2015.
[6] Matthiae 1997: 32

A

depicted image in such a way. The scene is composed with great finesse and a perfect symmetry: the king, the tallest figure, is in the centre, and on both his left and his right are six figures and a horse. Behind the king, an Assyrian official holds four enemies by rope, followed by an Assyrian holding a horse by its reins. The king also holds a rope in his left hand, to which are attached five defeated enemies, again followed on this side by an Assyrian pulling a horse by its reins. One must further note that in his left hand the king is also holding a rod, so the rope buckle and the royal rod are superimposed on each other in a way that is reminiscent of a motif from the steles from the Gudea period and from the Hammurabi Code: the ring and the rod – the insignias of power[8]. And that is not by chance: when celebrating victory in a mountain country, the king also displays symbols of

FIGURE 4.2: STONE CULT PEDESTAL OF TUKULTI-NINURTA I. SOURCE: MATTHIAE 1997: 31-32.

B

the conquerors. The minimally preserved lower section allows us to see a human head in front of two horses' heads and part of a male head. The interpretation of these identifies the Assyrian king's face on the partial head, and the complete head preceding the horses being that of a royal dignitary. This interpretation is not called into question here; rather, one wishes to emphasise its origin. It is based on comparisons with Neo-Assyrian and perhaps proto-dynastic depictions. The former are the most pertinent in terms of style and composition, whereas the latter are much more distant from a stylistic as much as a representative viewpoint. This is already proof of the Middle Assyrian influence on the 1st millennium BC, even though these comparisons have often been made automatically, being used to seeing the king on his chariot in Neo-Assyrian bas-reliefs, and thus not paying attention to the fact that the most direct precursor dates back to the Middle Assyrian period.

On the stone Cult Pedestal attributed to Tukulti-Ninurta I (*Figure 4.2*), the base shows a war scene described by all the commentators as the king receiving enemies in a mountain region.[7] However, one cannot describe the

power which, in memory of the Mesopotamians, were intrinsically linked to the gods. These are the gods who give them to the 'just' kings: Zimri-Lim at Mari, Hammurabi at Babylon, the unknown king on the stele from Suse (*Figure 4.3*)– divine justification of war despite the dead and the farming losses… One can already see the links that this image has with the Neo-Assyrian depictions.

The seals do not show the image of a battle, of a struggle between human characters, but are in some cases about hunting[9] (*Figure 4.4*), which is the other motif of the warrior king.[10] The hunting images include the chariot,

[8] For more details on the stele from the Gudea period, discovered at Suse without any inscription (Paris, Louvre; preserved height 80 cm), see Matthiae 2000. For more on the ring and the rod, see lastly (with preceding bibliography) Albenda 2005; Collon 2007; Ornan 2005, 2007b, 2009.

[9] Harper *et alii* 1995: 65-66, fig. 26 ; Invernizzi 1992 : 156; Moortgat 1944.

[10] From the earliest hunting images (Uruk stele of the hunt, Uruk period, IM. 23477, of which a height of 80cm is preserved; stone bowl with a hunt scene in relief, BM 118466, height 7 cm), it has always been the king involved. This shows the very long continuity (from the 4th millennium BC to the 1st) of the scene that has only been able to survive the changes of people, languages and cultures because it precisely responds to the royal demands (and to the politico-religious

[7] Now in Istanbul Museum (n° 7802), Andrae 1935; Ornan 2009: 115-117.

FIGURE 4.3: STELE FROM SUSE (LOUVRE, SB 7). SOURCE: MATTHIAE 2000: 52.

which have been forsaken in the monumental relief.[11] So, in the Middle-Assyrian period the chariot takes its place in hunting scenes –not in war ones- and then in the I millennium BC it resumes in war scenes on monumental reliefs from Assurnasirpal onwards.

The Broken Obelisk (*Figure 4.5*) of Assur-bel-kala[12] (11th century BC), is very poorly preserved. There remains only 63cm of its top, thus part of the inscription which must have extended over most of the surface area and the almost complete image – only missing are the feet of the figures of the king holding his vanquished enemies by rope. The image is crueller than the one carved on the base of the altar two centuries earlier: here, in fact, the vanquished figures have a ring through their nose – humiliating treatment that links humans with animals. The Neo-Assyrian kings will be inspired by this when – some centuries later – they attach their conquered enemies to the city gates along with animals (bears, dogs, pigs).[13] On the Broken Obelisk there is another element that will inspire the kings of the 1st millennium BC: the depiction of a divinely presence in the form of symbols.[14] One notices thus the skilful composition of the scene: the king, the tallest figure, far on the left, presents his head at the same level as the divine symbols – a very rapid way, with just a glance, to show at what level to position him. In contrast, the vanquished are relegated to the far right of the scene, the two foremost coming up just to

310   **A**

B

FIGURE 4.4: HUNT SEALS SOURCE: HARPER *ET ALII* 1995: 65-66, FIG. 26 ; INVERNIZZI 1992 : n° 310.

representation of the king, also essential in justifying his power and social 'differences').

[For] more on the Middle Assyrian seals, see: a seal impression on a tablet found at Assur (Moortgat fig. 38f).

11 See here the contribution of Béatrice Muller.

12 Ornan 2007a and 2009: 117-118; Borker-Klhan 1982; Andrae 1935.

13 Dunanu, Samgunu and Aplaya were chained with a bear, in front of the "gate of the East and the West" of Arbela (Weidner 1932-33: 182, episode 26). Also the king of Arza was chained with a bear, a dog and a pork in front of a gate of Nineveh under Esarhaddon (Borger 1956: 50, Nin. A–F, Episode 7: iii 40-42). For further references see Villard 2008 and for iconographic sources see Matthiae 2009.

14 For Neo-Assyrian period see the relevant remarks of Ornan 2007b.

FIGURE 4.5: BROKEN OBELISK OF ASSUR-BEL-KALA (11TH CENTURY BC), FROM NINEVEH. SOURCE: MATTHIAE 1997: 33.

FIGURE 4.6: OLD BABYLONIAN TERRACOTTA REPRESENTING THE EPIPHANY OF GOD (PHILADELPHIE, PENN MUSEUM, Y.B.C. 10.035). SOURCE: OPIFICIUS 1961: N° 399.

the king's chest, the two behind to his waist, all of them with arms raised, imploring for pity, as on the altar base. In the centre of the scene, thus, is a gap separating the good from the bad, the righteous from the imploring – a separation sought to distance the cosmos (king) from chaos (the vanquished). And reappearing in this gap are the signs of power – the rope and the rod. Once again, by way of divine symbols and the insignia of power, the message that the scene conveys is the justification of war and the divine blessing of the righteous king who knew he had to confront his enemies, overcome them and thus enable civilisation to reign over the 'barbarians' – order over disorder.[15]

Outline of a syntax

Various media are used for war images in the Middle Assyrian period: an altar, a box, an obelisk, seals. However the techniques used are essentially sculpture and engraving. The chronology that places the pyxis and the altar earlier than the obelisk enables one to suggest a heightening of the 'ferocity' of the depiction of war: from the enemies killed and mistreated during combat (pyxis lid), there is a progression to the roping of the vanquished, who fear their fate to the extent of raising their arms to beg for pardon or pity (altar base), then ultimately on to the vanquished being treated like animals, the rope fixed through a ring in their nose (Broken Obelisk). One also appears to see a parallel heightening of the symbols of

divine benevolence vis-à-vis the king: from the insignias of power given by the gods (altar base) we arrive at the accumulation of such insignias together with divine symbols (Broken Obelisk).

Unfortunately, apart from the altar, the Middle Assyrian objects that depict war are all broken, so it becomes impossible to evaluate the extent of these images in their entirety.[16] But one can try at least to better interpret the altar. In fact all the commentaries consider separately the two images on the altar: the king between two pseudo-Gilgamesh standard bearers and the capturing of enemies. And yet the two scenes cannot be understood otherwise than together, even though the task is not easy because the main scene that appears on approximately fifty centimetres of the anterior face constitutes an *unicum*. This image has been interpreted as depicting the temple entrance with the two guards who protect it and who allude to the astral realm, either as heroes bound to Shamash or as temporary vessels of Ishtar. According to one other more plausible interpretation, the king here depicts a theme frequent in the terracotta finding from the Old Babylonian period, where the scene was used for the gods (*Figure 4.6*). By putting himself in divine place, the king thus alludes discreetly – but probably clearly to his public – if not to his divinity then at least to

---

[15] For the Neo-Assyrian period, see: Larsen 1979; Liverani 1979: 297-317; *Id.* 1980 and 2010; Liverani (ed) 2002; Matthiae 2014. For the importance of studying ancient propaganda to keep contemporary freedom and a clear look at current propaganda see the penetrating article of Liverani 1996.

[16] Cf. Matthiae 1969, 1989b, 1992, 2003 and 2015.

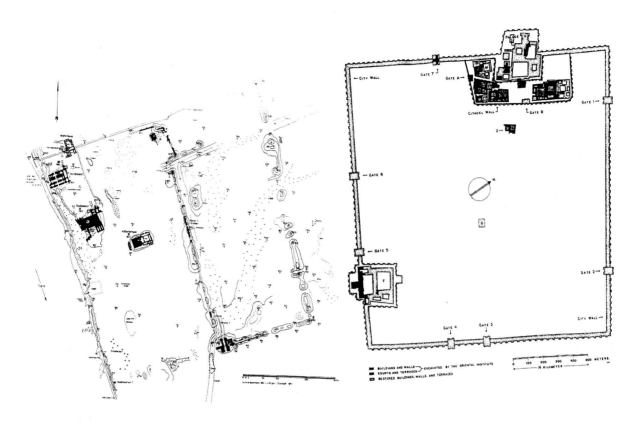

FIGURE 4.7: URBAN SETTINGS OF KAR-TUKULTI-NINURTA AND DUR-SHARRUKIN. SOURCE: ORIGINAL SETTING.

his exceptional status which places him above all men. Without denying this interpretation, which anyway I suggested some years ago, I think I can now complete it thanks to the scene depicted on the altar base. Thus on one side, there is the king at the temple entrance, physically present at the entrance to the temple of Ishtar, where the altar was discovered, but also symbolically invested with his full power, like the Old Babylonian god appearing at the entrance to his temple. And on the other hand, there is neither a battle, nor the reception of vanquished enemies, just their transportation through far-off, steeply rugged areas. It is thus possible that the altar is making reference to the celebration of a triumph during which the king, at the temple entrance –and, more significant, in the temple of the goddess of war- and invested with his supreme power, watches the parade of the vanquished people he has captured with his army, far from Assyria. Moreover, even if it is perhaps not about a triumph, Tukulti-Ninurta cites in his inscriptions the capture and enchaining of a conquered king.[17]

Aside from the altar, discovered in the temple of Ishtar at Assur, one can suggest the context in which the pyxis and obelisk are used, even if their original location has been forever lost. The pyxis, made in a royal craft workshop in Assur,[18] shows to what extent since the Middle Assyrian period the royal court felt itself to be affected by war,

its justification, almost its 'banalisation'.[19] The obelisk discovered at Nineveh must have been in a public place but unfortunately we do not know how high it was. And that is extremely important, as the sculptured image is only around forty centimetres high, so if the obelisk was very tall there was only one public that could look at it – the gods.[20] So the context and analysis of these Middle Assyrian works provide us with really unexpected information: royal propaganda spreads across the whole of human and divine society, with subtle difference in the messages according to the ability to receive them: the internal indoctrination of power (pyxis), highly visible public celebration (altar) and messages to the gods, involuntary accomplices in royal decisions (obelisk).

Relationships with the Iron Age

This way of creating nuances in royal messages[21] on the basis of which kind of public the work is primarily aimed at, is thus not a Neo-Assyrian innovation (and probably not a Middle Assyrian one either). But let us say that the insistence on war and the subtle differentiation of the royal message are first seen during the three last centuries of the second millennium BC. It is not only a passage of motifs and certainly also of style and of the media used: the Middle Assyrian influence on the first millennium BC goes much further, by including the new conception

---

[17]   And moreover there remains the epic of Tukulti-Ninurta, of which very little is known.
[18]   Matthiae 1997: 32.

[19]   Cancik-Kirschbaum 1997; Matthiae 1997: 32.
[20]   Cf. in this book the contribution of Ariel Bagg.
[21]   Matthiae 1994, 1996, 1998.

of royalty, the links with the gods, the considerations on strangers, the internal and external justifications of a society, part of whose wealth stems from the territories of others, in the spoils and gifts received from countries keen to distance themselves from the danger of attack. In this context, one should carefully reconsider the figure of Tukulti-Ninurta for he seems to have had great influence on the Neo-Assyrian kings: from the construction of a new capital city, from the extremely close similarity between the urban settings of Kar-Tukulti-Ninurta and Dur-Sharrukin (*Figure 4.7*) (even in the name),[22] to the defiance of the clergy, the iconographic subject matter and the fascination for Babylon…

References

Albenda, P. 2005. The Queen of the Night Plaque- A Revisit, JAOS 125: 171-190.

Andrae, W. 1935. *Die jüngeren Ischtar-Tempel in Assur*, WVDOG 58. Berlin.

Artzi, P. 1997. The Middle-Assyrian Kingdom as Precursor to the Assyrian Empire. In H. Waetzoldt and H. Hauptmann (eds), *Assyrien im Wandel der Zeiten. XXXIXe Rencontre Assyriologique Internationale, Heidelberg, 6.-10. Juli 1992*, Heidelberger Studien zum Alten Orient 6: 3-6. Heidelberg, Heidelberger Orientverlag.

Battini, L. 1994. La città quadrata: un modello urbano nella Mesopotamia del II e I millennio a. C.? *Orient Express 1994/2*: 49-50.

Battini, L. 2007. Quelques considérations sur la topographie de Babylone. *Ah Purattim* 2: 281-297.

Battini, L. 2014. Babylone entre mythe et réalité archéologique. In K. Zakharia (ed), *Babylone, Grenade : villes mythiques ; récits, réalités, représentations*, TMO: 71-84. Lyon.

Borger, R. 1956. *Die Inschriften Asarhaddons Königs von Assyrien*, AfO Beiheft 9. Graz.

Borker - Klähn, J. 1982. *Altorientalische Bildstelen und vergleichbare Felsreliefs I- II*. Mainz am Rhein.

Cancik-Kirschbaum, E. 1997. Rechtfertigung von politischem Handel in Assyrien im 13./12. Jh. v. Chr. In B. Pongratz-Leisten, H. Kühne and P. Xella (eds), *Ana shadi Labnani lù allik.Festschrift Wolfang Röllig*: 69-77. Kevelaer/Neukirchen-Vluyn.

Cancik-Kirschbaum, E. 2003. *Die Assyrer, Geschichte, Gesellschaft, Kultur*, Munich.

Cancik-Kirschbaum, E. 2012. Verwaltungstechnische Aspekte königlicher Repräsentation. In G. Wilhelm (ed), *Orgnization, Representation ans Symbols of Power in the Ancient Near Est. Proceedings of the 54th RAI at Würzburg, 20-25 July, 2008*: 33-49. Winona Lake, Eisenbrauns.

Champion, T. C. (ed) 1995. *Centre and Periphery: Comparative Studies in Archaeology*. London/NY, Routledge

Collon, D. 2007. The Queen under Attack—A Rejoinder. *Iraq* 69 : 43-51.

Drews, R. 1993. *The End of the Bronze Age: Changes in Warfare and the Catastrophe ca. 1200 BC*. Princeton.

Forest, J.-D. 2001. Compte rendu de Gil Stein, *Rethinking World-Systems. Diasporas, Colonies, and Interaction in Uruk Mesopotamia*, 1999, Tucson, The University of Arizona Press. *L'Homme* n. 160: 293-297.

Frahm, E. 2009. *Historische und historisch-literarische Texte*.WVDOG 121. Wiesbaden, Harrassowitz.

Grayson, A. K. 1990. *Assyrian Rulers of the Early First Millenium B.C. (1114-895 BC)*, RIMA 2.

Harper, P. O., Klengel-Brandt, E., Aruz, J. and Benzel K. (eds) 1995. *Discoveries at Ashur on the Tigris. Assyrian Origins. Antiquities in the Vorderasiatisches Museum, Berlin*, New York, Metropolitan Museum of Art Publication.

Invernizzi, A. 1992a. *Dal Tigri all'Eufrate, I. Sumeri e Accadi* (Studi e materiali di archeologia, 5), Firenze.

Invernizzi, A. 1992b. *Dal Tigri all'Eufrate. Babilonesi e Assiri* (Studi e materiali di archeologia, 5), Firenze.

Larsen, M. T. (ed) 1979. *Power and Propaganda. A Symposium on Ancient Empires*, Copenhagen Studies in Assyriology 7. Copenhagen.

Liverani, M. 1979. The Ideology of the Assyrian Empire. In M. T. Larsen (ed), *Power and Propaganda. A Symposium on Ancient Empires*, Copenhagen Studies in Assyriology 7 : 297-317. Copenhagen.

Liverani, M. 1980. Stereotipi della lingua 'altra' nell'Asia anteriore antica. *Vicino Oriente* 3: 15-31.

Liverani, M. 1984. The Growth of the Assyrian Empire on the Habur / Middle Euphrates Area: a New Paradigm. *Annales Archéologiques Arabes Syriennes* 34: 107-115.

Liverani, M. 1987. The collapse of the Near Eastern regional system at the end of the Bronze Age: the case of Syria. In M. Rowlands, M.T. Larsen and K. Kristiansen (eds), *Centre and Periphery in the Ancient World*: 66-73. Cambridge, Cambridge University Press.

Liverani, M. 1988. *Antico Oriente. Storia, economia, società*, Manuali Laterza 17. Roma-Bari, Laterza.

Liverani, M. 1989-1990. Scambi umani e scambi divini. *Scienze dell'Antichità* 3-4: 99- 101.

Liverani, M. 1995. Ideologia delle nuove fondazioni urbane in età neo-assira. In S. Mazzoni (ed), *Nuove fondazioni nel Vicino Oriente antico: realtà e ideologia. Atti del colloquio 4-6 dicembre 1991, Dipartimento di Scienze storiche del mondo antico, Sezione di egittologia e scienze storiche del Vicino Oriente, Università degli studi di Pisa*: 375-383. Pisa, Giardini.

Liverani, M. 1996. Ancient Propaganda and Historical Criticism. In J. S. Cooper and G. M. Schwartz (eds), *The Study of the Ancient Near East in the Twenty-First*

---

[22] Battini 1994, 2007 and 2014; Liverani 1995; Matthiae 1995;
[But] it is very probable that the template of Kar-Tuk and of Dur-Sharrukin, either directly or indirectly (via Kar-Tukulti-Ninurta) had been Babylon (Battini 1994), where the neo-Babylonian development seemingly copies the structure of the city from the twelfth century BC (Battini 2007 and 2014).

Century. The William Foxwell Albright Centennial Conference held at Johns Hopkins University in 1991: 283- 289. Winona Lake, Eisenbrauns.

Liverani, M. (ed) 2002. *Guerra santa e guerra giusta dal mondo antico alla prima età moderna*. Studi Storici, Rivista dell'Istituto Gramsci 43/3. Roma.

Liverani, M. 2004. Assyria in the Ninth Century: Continuity or Change? In G. Frame and L. S. Wilding (eds), *From the Upper Sea to the Lower Sea. Studies on the History of Assyria and Babylonia in Honour of A. K. Grayson*, Publications de l'Institut historique-archeologique neerlandais de Stamboul 101: 213-226. Leuven, Nederlands Instituut voor het Nabije Oosten.

Liverani, M. 2010. 'Untruthful Steles': Propaganda and Reliability in Ancient Mesopotamia. In S. C. Melville and A. L. Slotsky (eds), *Opening the Tablet Box: Near Eastern Studies in Honor of Benjamin R. Foster*, Culture and History of the Ancient Near East 42: 229-244. Leiden, Brill.

Masetti-Rouault, M.-G. 1998. Syriens et Assyriens dans la Djézire, XIVe-IXe siècle av. J-C. *Subartu* IV/2: 223-242.

Masetti-Rouault, M.-G. 2005. Conceptions de l'Autre en Mésopotamie ancienne: Barbarie et Différence, entre refus et intégration. *Cahiers Kubaba VII, Barbares et civilisés dans l'antiquité*: 121-141.

Masetti-Rouault, M.-G. and Rouault, O. (eds), forthcoming. *Après l'Empire: crise de l'État et de la Monarchie en Mésopotamie du Nord et en Anatolie (XIIIème- Xème siècles av. J.-C)/ After the Empire : Crisis of the State and of the Monarchy in Northern Mesopotamia and in Anatolia (XIIIth-Xth centuries BC)*, Actes du Colloque International de Lyon 2003.

Matthiae, P. 1969. La problematica dell'indagine storico-artistica. In M. Liverani (ed), *La Siria nel Tardo Bronzo*: 47-60. Roma.

Matthiae, P. 1989a. Old Syrian Ancestors of Some Neo-Assyrian Figurative Symbols of Kingship. In *Archaeologia iranica et orientalis. Miscellanea in honorem Louis Vanden Berghe*: 367-391. Gent, Peeters.

Matthiae, P. 1989b. Masterpieces of Early and Old Syrian Art: Discoveries of the 1988 Ebla Excavations in a Historical Perspective. *Proceedings of the British Academy* 75: 25-56.

Matthiae, P. 1992. Figurative Themes and Literary Texts. In P. Fronzaroli (ed), *Literature and Literary Language at Ebla*: 219-241. Firenze.

Matthiae, P. 1993. The Representation of the Natural Space from Khorsabad to Nineveh. In M. Liverani (ed), *Convegno internazionale 'La Geografia dell'Impero neoassiro', Roma 10-12 novembre 1993*.

Matthiae 1994. *Il sovrano e l'opera. Arte e poter nella Mesopotamia antica*. Roma-Bari, Laterza.

Matthiae, P. 1996. *L'arte degli Assiri. Cultura e forma del rilievo storico*. Roma.

Matthiae, P. 1997. *La Storia dell'arte dell'Oriente Antico. Vol. III: I Primi Imperi e i Principati del Ferro*. Milano, Electa.

Matthiae, P. 1998. *Ninive*. Milano, Electa.

Matthiae, P. 2000. *La Storia dell'arte dell'Oriente Antico. Vol. II: Gli Stati territoriali*. Milano, Electa.

Matthiae, P. 2003. History of Art in Ancient Near Eastern Archaeology: Problems and Perspectives. CMAO -Contributi e Materiali di Archeologia Orientale 9: 3-13.

Matthiae, P. 2009. Le immagini del trionfo : arte storica in Egitto e in Mesopotamia. *Mare internum : archeologia e culture del mediterraneo* n.1: 33-53.

Matthiae, P. 2010. The Seal of Ushra-Samu, Official of Ebla and Ishkhara's Iconography. In S. C. Melville and A. L. Slotsky (eds), *Opening the Tablet Box: Near Eastern Studies in Honor of Benjamin R. Foster*, Culture and History of the Ancient Near East 42: 271-290. Leiden, Brill.

Matthiae, P. 2012. Subject Innovations in the Khorsabad Reliefs and Their Political Meaning. In Giovanni B. Lanfranchi, Daniele Morandi Bonacossi, Cinzia Pappi (eds), *Leggo ! Studies Presented to Frederick Mario Fales on the Occasion of His 65th Birthday*: 477-497. Wiesbaden, Harrassowitz Verlag.

Matthiae, P. 2014. Image, Ideology, and Politics: a Historical Consideration of the Message of Neo-Assyrian Reliefs. In S. Gaspa, A. Greco and D. Morandi Bonacossi (eds), *From Source to History : Studies on Ancient Near Eastern Worlds and Beyond* : 387-404. Münster, Ugarit-Verlag.

Matthiae, P. 2015. *Distruzioni, saccheggi e rinascite. Gli attacchi al patrimonio artistico dall'antichità all'Isis*. Roma.

May, N. N. 2012. Triumph as an Aspect of the Neo-Assyrian Decorative Program. In G. Wilhelm (ed), *Orgnization, Representation ans Symbols of Power in the Ancient Near Est*. Proceedings of the 54th RAI at Würzburg, 20-25 July, 2008 : 461-488. Winona Lake, Eisenbrauns.

D. Morandi, "Stele e statue reali assire: localizzazione, diffusione e implicazioni ideologiche", *Mesopotamia* 23, 1988, 105-155.

Moortgat, A. 1943. Assyrische Glyptik des 12. Jahrhunderts. *ZA* 14: 23-44.

Ornan, T. 2007a. Who is Holding the Lead Rope? The Relief of the Broken Obelisk. *Iraq* 69: 59-72.

Ornan, T. 2007b, The Godlike Semblance of a King. In J. Cheng and M. Feldman M. (eds), *Ancient Near Eastern Art in Context : Studies in Honor of Irene J. Winter by Her Students*. Culture and History of the Ancient Near East 26: 161-178. Leiden, Brill.

Ornan, T. 2009. In the Likeness of Man, Reflections on the Anthropocentric Perception of the Divine in Mesopotamian Art, in B. Nevling Porter (ed), *What is a God? Anthropomorphic and Non-Anthropomorphic Aspects of Deity in Ancient Mesopotamia* (The Casco Assyriological Bay Institute Transactions 2): 93–151. Winona Lake, Eisenbrauns.

Pittman, H. 1996. The White Obelisk and the Problem of Historical Narrative in the Art of Assyria. *The Art Bulletin* 78: 334-355.

Pittman, H. 1997. Unwinding the White Obelisk. In H. Waetzoldt and H. Hauptmann (eds), *Assyrien im Wandel der Zeiten. XXXIXe Rencontre Assyriologique Internationale, Heidelberg, 6.-10. Juli 1992*, Heidelberger Studien zum Alten Orient 6: 347-354. Heidelberg, Heidelberger Orientverlag.

Rowlands, M., Larsen, M. T. and Kristiansen, K. (eds), 1987. *Centre and Periphery in the Ancient World.* Cambridge, Cambridge University Press.

Shafer A. (2007) Assyrian Royal Monuments on the Periphery: Ritual and the Making of Imperial Space. In J. Cheng and M. H. Feldman (eds), *Ancient Near Eastern Art in Context: Studies in Honor of Irene J. Winter by Her Students*, CHANE 26: 133-159.

Stein, G. 1999. *Rethinking World-Systems. Diasporas, Colonies, and Interaction in Uruk Mesopotamia.* Tucson, The University of Arizona Press.

Villard, P. 2008. Les ceremonies triomphales en Assyrie. In Ph. Abrahami and L. Battini (eds), *Les armées du Proche-Orient ancient (IIIe-Ier mill. Av. J.-C.)*, BAR 1855: 257-270. Oxford, Archeopress.

Ward and Sharp Joukowsky (eds) 1992. *The Crisis Years: the 12th Century BC from beyond the Danube to the Tigris.* Dubuque.

Weidner, E. F. 1932-33. Assyrische Beschreibungen der Kriegs-Reliefs Assurbânaplis. *AfO* 8: 175-203.

"Losing One's Head". Some Hints on Procedures and Meanings of Decapitation in the Ancient Near East

Rita Dolce*

The expression that gives this paper its title is employed, in current and consolidated usage, to describe various, sometimes conflicting, states in which an individual may find themselves: we speak of "losing one's head" as a result of great grief, falling in love, an excess of anger or a traumatic event of some kind, physical or psychological, and so forth. The expression is thus transposed from its primary meaning, referring to a concrete condition of extreme crudeness, to others relating to a temporary or permanent lack of the mental faculties. However, all these meanings contain within themselves a significance inherent *ab origine* in the condition of someone who finds himself "losing his head", in the metaphorical or literal sense, and which refers to a form of extraneousness, of alienation, in a word the "loss of self-control".

Within the scope of this conference on the Iconography of war in the Syro-Mesopotamian world, the theme of decapitation in times of war holds a special place in the visual communication of the procedures that precede, accompany or end armed conflicts. It also has a lasting impact on the figurative accounts to which I intend to draw attention and on those written accounts which will be referred to here only when they seem particularly relevant to this analysis.

I will thus document this topic in a broad chronological perspective that aims to highlight some conditions, relations and values characterizing this specific act in times of war.

During my research I have developed a conviction that in the figurative cultures of the ancient Near East decapitation cannot be compared to other forms/ procedures of violence inflicted on the human body, such as dismemberment, as other scholars have claimed:[1] decapitation is originally, and perhaps always, a separate procedure, with complex meanings linked to the core of the individual and of his energies and power.[2]

The loss of the head is certainly an incontrovertible act of annihilation of the enemy, as many would agree, but that is not all: it is the only definitive way of reducing the other to something inanimate, taking further a suggestion made in the past,[3] and, that is, without the breath of life. This immediately raises a first issue: were further treatments inflicted on the bodies of enemies deprived of their head and if so what were they?; are they assimilated to otherwise dismembered bodies or to intact bodies piled up in heaps for "burial" (with earth and burned) or not?

The most extensive documentation, that of the Neo-Assyrian period, frequently depicts completely anonymous headless bodies next to intact bodies floating in rivers or lying on the ground (*Figure 5.1*); by contrast, burial mounds, unfortunately rare in images over three millennia (*Figure 5.2*), whilst they recur in the Assyrian sources even before the Neo-Assyrian empire,[4] do not appear to involve a similar treatment for headless corpses.

Here I will mention only one celebrated example of the countless instances provided by the documentation from ancient Egypt: the depiction on the Narmer Palette. On the verso, ten naked enemies, decapitated and bound, perhaps supine, each have their own head placed between their legs.[5] This is a peculiar procedure that does not appear to be depicted in the figurative codes for visual communication on similar subjects in the context of warfare in the Near East of the III millennium BC and beyond.

It may be that the piles of SH in the Neo-Assyrian reliefs[6] act as "parts for the whole" and in some way replace heaps of bodies in the images. However, it should be noted that in this period the expression "heaps of enemy corpses" or part thereof, does not imply their burial, but rather their elimination by natural agents or burning, an explicit warning to enemies and a peremptory solution for the fallen.

---

* University of Roma TRE.

This paper presented in Lyon in 2012 is part of a research on the topic that has converged in the Author's volume *"Perdere la Testa".Aspetti e valori della decapitazione nel Vicino Oriente Antico*, Roma 2014".
The abbreviation SH in the text and notes stands for Severed Head(s).
[1] Talalay 2004: 139; Minunno 2008a: 248-249, though the head is considered of special value; Minunno 2008b.
[2] This procedure also involves images of statues of both mortals and deities: see Dolce 2016.

[3] Cf. Bonneterre 1997: 559-560.
[4] Already with Tukulti-Ninurta I: Richardson 2007: 197. Indeed, this practice and its recurrence in the sources of the III millennium BC have already been noted by Gelb 1973: 73-74, regarding royal inscriptions of the ensi of Lagash and of certain Akkadian kings. The spectacular habit of "piling up enemy corpses" also recurs in Eblaite texts of the Early Syrian Period, and in Mesopotamia until the Neo-Assyrian Period when severed heads, as parts for the whole, are frequently depicted in heaps; for further considerations see Dolce 2014: 243.
[5] Kaploni 2002: 468-469, fig. 29.11; according to Köhler (2002: 499 and ff.) Narmer is the first king of the I dynasty of Egypt, the predecessor of Hor-Aha, on the basis of the discovery of two seals in the necropolis of Abydos (Köhler 2002: 499).
[6] Novotny and Watanabe 2008: fig. 8; Barnett et alii 1998: pl. 193.

FIGURE 5.1: NEO-ASSYRIAN BAS RELIEFS

Returning to the uniqueness of the action in question and its effects, decapitation is distinct from all other mutilations, envisaged and inflicted, which do not in themselves entail the loss of life (severing hands and limbs, the tongue, the nose, the ears, or even the testicles); and which thus involve a different level of alienation/disabling of the enemy, in fact and meaning.

In visual language, in contrast to the anonymous nature of headless bodies, the head detached from its body is a "desired object", so to speak: an object at the mercy not only of those who have committed the act but also of others, as will be seen below. There is a shared participation and interaction between various living subjects in the vicissitudes of the severed head (with further acts being committed).

The act of decapitation

We will begin with the act itself, which in the most eloquent images can be perceived as an execution already in the III mill. BC, sometimes a ceremonious one on the Neo-Assyrian reliefs.[7] However, it has resonances at least from prehistory if, in the recent re-examination of the paintings in two houses at Çatal-Hüyük (*Figure 5.3*),[8] the birds of prey attacking headless corpses whose severed heads can be identified with the skulls treated and placed in the same rooms, is interpreted as a celebration of victories over enemies rather than as a funerary practice linked to ancestors.[9] Were this the case, the SH, appropriately treated and conserved, would be a form of possession and display- likely accessible only to

---

[7] Moortgat 1969: pl.134 (detail); Barnett 1976: pl. XXIV.

[8] Testart 2008: 34-36, fig. 2.

[9] In contrast to Mellaart 1967: 167-169, fig. 47, pls. 45, 48-49.

FIGURE 5.2: DETAIL OF THE STELE OF VULTURES (III MILL. BC)

FIGURE 5.3: EXAMPLE OF PAINTINGS FROM ÇATAL HÖYÜK

the elites- of the head of the enemy; but we will return to this issue later.

Decapitation also seems to be evoked in the proto-historical glyptics from Uruk,[10] in the images of the imminent execution of kneeling prisoners, tied up near execution blocks.

Severing the head is nonetheless a procedure which was widely employed, judging from the most extensive visual evidence, that of the Neo-Assyrian period and judging from the epigraphical sources covering three millennia; it is worth mentioning those from Amorrite Mari,[11] those from Assyria generally and of course the countless references in the annals of the Neo-Assyrian sovereigns.[12]

So we should ask ourselves the question, not immediately obvious: to what extent was decapitation reserved for "some" enemies: was this a selective practice or not? Although when we do have texts from various kingdoms spanning three millennia which explicitly mention cutting off the head of illustrious individuals – from powerful enemy kings to rulers of kingdoms of middling importance and high-ranking individuals[13] - the exaltation of the act inflicted on these specific subjects is evident, we should also be aware that, at least in Assyria,

in images the heaps of SH piled up next to valuable furnishings and weapons (*Figure 5.4*) are assimilated to the booty of war and its counting.

In my opinion this is an important indicator of the "economic value" of SH, perhaps even more cogent than the numerous mentions of hundreds of decapitations which recur in the royal inscriptions, even before the Neo-Assyrian period.[14]

The act of displaying

It is worth noting that the SH is proudly displayed by victors already during the III mill. BC. However, this is not the case in the figurative sources from Mesopotamia, where this practice seems to be unknown in law,[15] although SH appear in those from Syria, at Ebla (*Figure 5.5*), alongside the textual data from the Archives of Royal Palace G on the practice of decapitation and subsequent procedures, which will be discussed below.

The same semantic/figurative code of the exhibition of SH held by the hair by Eblaite victors recurs more than a millennium later in numerous cases: from the orthostates of the Long Wall of Sculpture at Carchemish to the

---

[10] Brandes 1979, pl. 13.
[11] Jean 1950: 74-77, no. 33 and subsequent up-dates in Charpin 1993 on the episode of Ishme-Addu, king of Ashnakkum (in the Khabur area) who had himself decapitated out of shame for having betrayed the king of Mari to ally himself with the latter's defeated enemies; cf. for further details Charpin 1988: 41-42; Charpin 1994 provides a collection of passages from the Mari texts on severed heads indicative of their dual significance, as a homage to the allied king or as an insult to the enemy king: for this issue I refer below in this study; Durand 1998: 176-177, no. 559; Durand 2000: 322-323, no. 1144.
[12] Already with Tiglathpileser I in the XIIth c. BC, written sources report hundreds of SH, proof that this practice was widespread: Glassner 2006: 50; according to Richardson 2007: 197, piles of SH begin, first, with this king but, I would add, not in the images: cf. Dolce 2004: 121 referring to the available visual documentation and not just to textual documents; for the practice reported in Neo-Assyrian texts see Richardson 2007: 196-197.
[13] Such as in sources from Ebla, Mari, and mainly in the annals of the Assyrian sovereigns: see below.

[14] See above and note 12.
[15] As we are reminded by Glassner 2006: 52.

FIGURE 5.4: HEAPS OF SH PILED UP NEXT TO VALUABLE FURNISHINGS AND WEAPONS, NEO-ASSYRIAN PERIOD.

scattered reliefs from Til Barsip up to the sequence of at least six carved slabs from Tell Taynat.[16]

I note that at Tell Taynat the heads displayed are smaller than those of the soldiers (*Figure 5.6*), in line with the style prevalent in Neo-Assyrian reliefs; and that the bodies to which they belonged still lie on the ground, where the victors are, indicating that the act has just taken

place. The latter circumstance is not to be found in what is hitherto the most ancient example from Ebla and is no longer verifiable for the other Syro-Anatolian reliefs just mentioned.[17] I would currently consider it a variant that, besides the act itself, also substantiates the ownership of the head; these data frequently do not appear so precise even in the very large sample of Neo-Assyrian reliefs, with the exception of elite figures[18] or decapitations as they take place. Certainly the small size of the heads reflects the same conventions applied at Ebla, but with different dimensional values: in the case of Ebla I have suggested for some time that oversized heads, again held by the hair and displayed, indicate the high status of the decapitated enemies, whilst the smaller heads heaped up in baskets belong to "others", in accordance with a visual code that aims to stress the differing value of the

---

[16] Woolley and Barnett 1952: 166, pls. B44-46; Orthmann 1971: 33-34, 47, 60, 503, 535, 537-538, pls. 25a, b, 54b, c, 55b. A third slab from Til Barsip, so worn as to be almost illegible, is considered by Orthmann 1971: 47, pl. 53a, comparable to the other two for the theme of war, in the form of a rider and his equid of which a part can be identified. In my opinion this subject seems similar to that on the slab from Zincirli (pl. 55b). Of particular interest are the fragmentary sculpted orthostates, seven in total, with a sequence of soldiers holding the SH of the defeated by the hair in their right hands; at least six of these orthostates were improperly reused as flagstones and may originally have belonged to the phase of the so-called Third Building period and to the reign of Tiglathpileser III: Harrison 2005: 26, fig. 1. The surveys conducted at this site between the late 20th and early 21st century have already shown the importance of Taynat as the most extensive town in the Amuq plain in the III mill. BC and we can suggest that it played a leading political role in the region within Syria at the time of the rise of Old Syrian Ebla: Batiuk et alii 2005: 177-178. This historical reconstruction has recently continued with the resumption of excavations and the landscape archaeology project of the University of Toronto; the data emerging concern the widespread presence of remains between the EB IVA and B and the uncovering of a large complex existing during the EB IVB, and contemporary with late Early Syrian Ebla; furthermore, the evidence provided by the Ebla archive texts on the toponyms relating to sites in the Amuq may help to draw an outline of the region already in the III mill. BC and to see in Taynat perhaps the most important town in the Amuq at the time of Ebla: Welton et alii 2011: 149-150, 152.

[17] See note 16, including Carchemish and Zincirli; Woolley and Barnett 1952: 166 and pls. B44-46, especially B46a. The poor and grainy nature of the photographs makes it difficult to identify bodies on the ground; clearly visible are the series of fractures and recompositions of the four surviving limestone slabs which, according to the author, belonged to a series at least twice as long; the four lost slabs/orthostates may have been made of marble rather than limestone and reused at a later period: Woolley and Barnett 1952: 166, note 7.

[18] Particularly incisive among the numerous studies of this issue, the considerations on the identity of the decapitated individual in Bahrani 2004: 116-117; Bahrani 2008: 55, 201 and ff. especially; and by Watanabe 2004: 107-114; Watanabe 2008: 602, 604, regarding the Elamite king Teuman and his son Tammaritu. Recurrences and significances of images of the decapitation of important individuals in the Neo-Assyrian period are also analysed in Dolce 2004: 126-129.

FIGURE 5.5: SOLDIERS BRINGING DECAPITATED HEADS. FROM EBLA, III MILL. BC

FIGURE 5.6: SOLDIERS BRINGING DECAPITATED HEADS. FROM TELL TAYNAT, I MILL. BC

"desired object"; this language does not reappear in the same form in the Near Eastern documentation.[19]

Indeed, in the many similar images on the reliefs from the Assyrian capitals and provincial towns, the heads

displayed are mainly very small, sometimes close to life size, but never oversized, though we can in any case assume an intentional distinction between one type and the other. However, the actual qualitative distinction between SH seems to be made in the more or less spectacular description/episodic account of the individual event, supported by the inscriptions; this is

---

[19] Dolce 2006: 39.

what makes the difference. I therefore ask myself if the smaller heads heaped up in the baskets carried by Eblaite soldiers are not equivalent, in the expressive syntax of this theme, to the heaping up of SH for counting in the documentation of the reliefs of the Neo-Assyrian period.

It seems that from its first known attestation in the III mill. BC we are dealing with an extensive and widespread, and not merely selective, practice of decapitation.

Destinations of the SH: some pieces of evidence

We have just mentioned the most frequent aim: the "desired object" as booty. In this case, the actions of the active protagonists, the victors, are numerous and complementary in the Assyrian documentation: the removal of SH and their transportation to the place of "counting"[20] (*Figure 5.7*) with several subjects participating in this procedure with different roles, from soldiers to scribes, to high-ranking officials as in the case represented in the paintings from Til Barsip.[21]

Another destination of heads was to become food for birds of prey, as in the so-called vultures stele from Lagash of the mid III mill. and likely already manifest again from the proto-historical period in the glyptics from Uruk (*Figure 5.8*)[22]. Here it presents a peculiar

FIGURE 5.7: REMOVAL OF SH AND THEIR TRANSPORTATION TO THE PLACE OF "COUNTING". NEO-ASSYRIAN PERIOD.

character that requires reflection: the attack is on the heads of prisoners who are still alive, preceded in my opinion by their leader, and is made by lion-headed birds of prey; could this be an evocation of a mythical theme within the representation of an account of victory over an enemy? We might recall the presence of lion-headed eagles on the Ebla victory panel, daringly interpreted by Matthiae[23] as the destructive force unleashed on the defeated (identified with the human-headed bulls).

Generally speaking, we can add that the relationship between birds of prey and heads, and perhaps between birds of prey and defeated enemies, goes back much further, to the Neolithic period, judging from the complex documentation on the walls of two buildings at Catal Hüyük mentioned above. Here the deposition of skulls, treated to preserve them, is always associated with rooms decorated only with large depictions of flying birds of prey assaulting headless bodies (*Figure 5.9*).[24] If Testart's well-argued theory is correct[25] this complex apparatus, which in my opinion can be described as figurative-historical-communicative, would be the permanent celebration of a victory following conflicts[26] and the skulls in the painted houses may belong to important decapitated enemies rather than to valiant ancestors.[27] This would mean that we are dealing with one of the most archaic codified forms of display/ exhibition.[28]

This connection is made explicit in the aforementioned "vultures stele" (*Figure 5.10*): here the "two-person match" involves flying vultures grabbing the heads and carrying them elsewhere, just like the soldiers who grab the heads and take them elsewhere, for the counting of the booty and other purposes. This is yet another version of the display of the "desired object": for every conqueror, for counting, for sensory pleasure in the form of food.[29]

---

[23] Matthiae 1995: 277-278.

[24] Testart 2008: 33 and ff., figs. 2, 3.

[25] Despite the heated debate triggered by this hypothesis and the controversial theories proposed by various scholars (cf. Paléorient 35/2009); of the collected papers we cite that by Hodder 2009: 109-111, especially for the remark that the skulls intentionally removed from the body belong to both men, women and infants and therefore cannot be considered to belong to warriors as a whole; and the paper by Forest 2009: 113-115, who accepts the hypothesis of Testart 2008 but at the same time does not associate the vultures with the practice of decapitation, considering them simply signs of death. The visual and other documentation in the cultures of the Ancient Near East seems to me to prove the relationship between SH and birds of prey in the context of war.

[26] Testart 2008: 35-39 especially.

[27] The second hypothesis, that these were skulls of ancestors now the object of worship, is an alternative that Testart keeps open (Testart 2008: 39).

[28] Other aspects of this issue are dealt with in my ongoing research.

[29] In agreement on the historical nature of the events represented on the vultures stele are Miglus (2008: 231), Nadali (2007: 351 and ff., 355 especially), Alster (2003-2004) and others, including the present author; already Winter (1985: 4-6, 11 and ff., 17, 19 especially) was of this opinion. The objection by Miglus (2008: 231-232) that the king could not fight in the front line is countered by the fact that on the stele the actions are developed in the form of highlights and that

---

[20] This operation only seemingly concerns the counting of the SH, as S. Donadoni has for some time perceptively argued: Donadoni 1985: 502, stating that it aims rather at displaying the condition of inferiority of the enemy compared to the solidity of the other's victory; this theory is reported in Nadali 2001-2003: 64, note 41, who notes (*Id.* 2001-2003: 64, 69), in agreement with most scholars, that the counting serves to render eternal the death of the enemy in everyone's eyes and also to exalt the personal victory of the king.

[21] Thureau-Dangin and Dunand, 1936: pl. LII; for some considerations on the pictures from this site see Dolce 2004: 125-129, figs.10, 11.

[22] Boehmer 1999: fig. 64 .

FIGURE 5.8: HEADS BECAME FOOD FOR BIRDS OF PREY, EXAMPLE FROM URUK GLYPTIC.

FIGURE 5.9: HEADS BECAME FOOD FOR BIRDS OF PREY, EXAMPLE FROM ÇATAL HÖYÜK.

It should also be noted that another renowned monument, the Sargon stele, apparently does not develop this theme in a similar way;[30] the same is true of the royal glyptics from Mari[31] on the seal impressions of the lugal Ishqi-Mari,[32] where birds of prey are attacking parts of the faces of the defeated, naked and lifeless on the ground. Images comparable to those topping the Eannatum stele are not hitherto known in the figurative culture of the second half of the III mill.BC.

Two works showing these two different levels of visual communication, each likely connected with different meanings of the actions, can be found over time. One is the stele of king Dadusha (*Figure 5.11*) of the first half of the II mill. BC, where the heads of SH of nine illustrious warriors,[33] standing at the bottom of the monument as in

generally speaking, even where he does not put himself in danger, his role as a protagonist is evident, as on Neo-Assyrian reliefs and the corresponding textual narratives.

[30] Nigro 1997: fig. 12: the vultures, together with starving dogs, attack the bodies of enemies on the ground apparently not deprived of their heads; the value attributed some time ago to this scene, rightly considered "realistic"(Nigro 1997: 377), in my opinion in itself marks the ideological distance separating the flying vultures with their "treasure" on the Eannatum monument from the earthly slaughter perpetrated in the Sargon version.

[31] These represent precious figurative and textual evidence (see note 32) on seal-impressions on bullae for sealing doors from official and royal contexts of the City II, the renaissance of the city and the kingdom, whose historical and chronological definition remains complex, but can be dated to the late Early Dynastic Period and the Early Akkad: see Beyer (2007: 246 and ff., 249-253) for the seal-impressions of Ishqi-Mari.

[32] Beyer 2007: 249, note 63, as attested by the short inscription with name and title.

[33] These individuals are not mentioned in the inscription and may be relatives of the defeated king: cf. Charpin 2004: 158; Nadali 2008: 134, note 33. The proposal that there were nine rather than ten heads, convincingly advanced by Charpin (2004: 158, note 14) is in agreement

FIGURE 5.10: FLYING VULTURES GRABBING THE HEADS OF ENEMIES, III MILL. BC (STELE OF VULTURES).

the Sargon stele, are attacked by small birds of prey. The other is the main representation on one of the slabs from the throne room of Assurnasirpal II[34] at Nimrud, where a bird of prey flies majestically, transporting the SH of what may be an illustrious enemy, flanking the triumphal chariot and keeping pace with it.

Finally, passages of the royal Neo-Assyrian inscriptions (from Assurnasirpal II to Salmanaser III) deserve some consideration, starting from the stele of Eannatum, regarding the recurrent metaphor of victors as birds of prey falling on their victims;[35] this would support the hypothesis advanced here, that the vultures replicate the actions of victors in specific iconographical formulations.

Numerous other destinations are reserved for SH and in some cases allow us to associate the "desired object" with more or less important individuals, given the circumstances of the event.

I mention only some cases among the most frequently recurring in the textual sources between the III and I Mill. BC, in Mesopotamia and in Syria with their counterparts in the visual documentation where available:

a) As gifts to the most important king by other sovereigns, notables of the kingdom or vassals.[36]

b) as tangible proof and glorious spoils for victors (connected to the previous instance or otherwise). SH are suspended from trees, both outside towns and indoors in courtyards and palaces, documented mainly in the Neo-Assyrian sources.[37] SH are displayed on the gates and walls of the city, already quoted in the most ancient texts, those from Ebla.[38]

c) as a macabre homage to the enemy king from his rival in the form of the head of his loyal ally.[39]

The moving SH

I note that many of the procedures linked to decapitation share the transportation from one place to another of the SH, both in the textual and visual sources.[40]

---

with the mention in a text from Mari of nine kings defeated in exactly the same year as this event. Who are these men?: the inscription mentions, after the king himself Bunu-Eshtar, defeated and decapitated, the defeated king and his allies, but without naming them, on whom Dadusha "has extended silence": Charpin 2004: 154; in the images we may therefore be dealing with one or the other, or with warrior members of the royal family of Qabrâ, as I proposed above; on the other hand, we know that some members of the family of the defeated king were spared by Dadusha (Charpin 2004: 165-166, note 53) though he did not make corresponding mention of this in the inscription on the stele. The latter circumstance can be explained as a voluntary omission from the inscription of an "act of mercy" on the part of the victor whilst it emphasises the aggressive aspects of the victory.

[34] Meuszyński 1981: pl. 2 (detail slab B6).
[35] Jean 2005: 88-89.

[36] From the Royal Archive of early Syrian Ebla and Amorrite Mari: TM.75.G.10219; TM.75.G.1902: Archi 1998: 388-389; TM.75.G.1741: Archi 2010: 32; Charpin 1993: 170; also in Archi 1998: 388; Charpin 1994: 52, n. 59. This type of homage also recurs in the Assyrian texts, as a "variant" on the tribute of SH to the victorious king "thrown at his feet", directly before his chariot and therefore outdoors: Glassner 2006: 48 and references; Albenda 1986: 89, pl. 111.
[37] Descriptions of these procedures can be found in the inscriptions of Assurnasirpal II: Grayson 1991: 201 and ff., no. 101.1 i.64, i.118, ii.18-19.ii.71-72; Assurnasirpal II on this fate in Grayson 1976: 132, no. 1(563); see also Archi 1998: 386.
[38] Archi 1990: 103, note 7; Archi 1998: 391 (TM.75.G.2429); Archi 2005: 89-90, note 28; the decapitation of this individual is confirmed by the ongoing research of M.V. Tonietti, whom I thank for the information. A different case appears to be that of a certain Iram-damu, a man of Dubadu, who was fixed "on the gate of Današ," a small satellite town of Ebla, (TM.75.G.2451): in fact it is not certain that he is an important figure, nor someone involved in war, according to Archi 2010: 32.
[39] References are found already in the texts from the II mill BC, when, Zazaya sends his enemy Ishme-Dagan the SH of the king of the city which he had besieged: Lafont 1988: 479-482 (52-53).
[40] The maximum expression is shown in the urgent progress of the

FIGURE 5.11: STELE OF THE KING DADUSHA, EARLY II MILL. BC

It seems worth noting the representative value of moving the SH from one place to other places, in different spatial and environmental conditions linked to conflicts.

SH are moved using human and other means of transportation; these include the victors transporting the "desired object" by hand, allies sending proof of the destruction of the enemy as a "gift" to its powerful recipient, birds of prey seizing it, or moving-displaying by cart.[41]

A last remark concerns the suggestion advanced some time ago that the main reason for decapitation was to provide oneself and others with the certainty that the enemy had been irreversibly annihilated before the world[42], giving one's own subjects a sense of security. The perceptive suggestion advanced by Glassner based on the mythical literature, takes this theory further, stating that the SH, once it becomes so, deprived of energies concentrated against the enemy, emanates an inverse, propitiatory force with apotropaic effects;[43] were this the case, the SH displayed on trees, on the gates and walls of defeated cities and victorious capitals and, first and foremost, that in the "garden of Eden" of the Palace of Assurbanipal could be read in a different light, pervaded by a ritual cathartic rather than horrific meaning.

Current research focusing specifically on the disfigurement of faces and the decapitation of statues,[44] and the recent collective study on the destruction of images and written texts in the ancient Near East contribute to broadening approaches to the meaning of decapitation both of humans beings and human and divine statues and to debate on the prevailing opinion that this act is motivated by political and ideological factors.[45]

---

head of Teumman in the space and time of the epic account of the battle of Til-Tuba, grasped from different perspectives by Bahrani 2004: 116 and ff.; Bahrani 2008: 54-55; and Watanabe 2008: 602 and ff.

[41]   As evoked in the saga of Teumman and already present in the royal glyptics from Mari-City II on war themes: Beyer 2007: 249-253, figs. 17, 18; here the head of the defeated enemy is transported and displayed on the cart of the victors with the effect, in my opinion, of achieving a striking visual impact rather than "a common detail" in Mesopotamian representations of the theme as is believed by Miglus 2008: 234. Regarding the cart, the observation by Watanabe 2008: 602 and note 6, that the cart used to transport the head of the defeated king Teumman was properly Elamite in my opinion suggests further aspects: that of a double booty, the cart and the SH of Teumann, and a double insult: the royal head displayed on his own cart on the part of the Assyrian victors. The visual message is different from that evident in similar circumstances on the royal victory seals of the late Early Dynastic period of the king of Mari Ishqi-Mari, mentioned above, where, in agreement with Beyer 2007: 251, 253 a SH appears on the cart, probably that of the defeated king, exhibited on the cart of the victorious king. I have thought for some time, on the basis of a reading of the narrative context, that carts represented in the celebrations of victories in war already in early dynastic Mesopotamia should be considered, symbolically and literally, the moving seat of victorious royalty: Dolce 2010: 50, note 28.
[42]   Richardson 2007: 198.
[43]   Glassner 2006: 50.The reference is to the mythical epos of the god Ninurta and others, and the vicissitudes suffered by the SH of monsters and heroes in general, culminating in their display on the doors of temples, often with an apotropaic function: Wiggermann 1992.
[44]   Kaim 2000; May 2010.
[45]   May 2012.

References

Albenda, P. 1986. *The Palace of Sargon King of Assyria.* Paris, *ERC*.

Alster, B. 2003-2004. Images and Text on the Stele of the Vultures. *AfO* 50: 1-10. Wien.

Archi, A. 1990. Données épigraphiques Eblaïtes et production artistique. *RA* 84: 101-105. Paris.

Archi, A. 1998. Two Heads for the King of Ebla. In M. Lubetski *et alii* (eds), *Boundaries of the Ancient Near Eastern World. A Tribute to Cyrus Gordon*: 386-396. Sheffield.

Archi, A. 2005. The Head of Kura - The Head of 'Adabal. *JNES* 64: 81-100. Chicago.

Archi, A. 2010. Men at War in the Ebla Period on the Unevenness of the Written Documents. In A. Kleinerman and J. Sasson (eds), *Why Should Someone Who Knows Something Conceal It? Cuneiform Studies In Honor of David I. Owen on His 70th Birthday*: 15-35. Bethesda.

Bahrani, Z. 2004. The King's Head. *Iraq* 46: 115-119. London.

Bahrani, Z. 2008. *Rituals of War*. New York.

Barnett, R. D. 1976. *Sculptures from the North Palace of Ashurbanipal at Nineveh (668-627 BC)*. London.

Barnett, R. D. *et alii* 1998. *Sculptures from the Southwest Palace of Sennacherib at Nineveh*. London.

Batiuk, S. *et alii* 2005. *The Amuq Valley Regional Projects Vol.I. Surveys in the Plain of Antioch and Orontes Delta, Turkey, 1995-2002*, OIP 131. Chicago.

Beyer, D. 2007. Les sceaux de Mari au IIIe millénaire: observations sur la documentation ancienne et les données nouvelles des Villes I et II. *Akh Purattim* 1: 231-260.

Boehmer, R. M. 1999. *Uruk. Früheste Siegelabrollungen*, AUWE 24. Mainz am Rhein.

Bonneterre, D. 1997. Surveiller, punir et se venger: la violence d'état à Mari. *MARI* 8: 537-561.

Brandes, M. A. 1979. *Siegelabrollungen aus dem Archaischen Bauschichten in Uruk-Warka, Teil I-II*. Wiesbaden.

Charpin, D. 1988. Les représentants de Mari à Ilân-Surâ. In D. Charpin *et alii*, *Archives Epistolaires de Mari* I/2, ARM XXVI/2: 31-137. Paris.

Charpin, D. 1993. Un souverain éphémère en Ida-Maraš: Išme-Addu d'Ašnakkum. *MARI* 7: 165-171.

Charpin, D. 1994. Une décollation mystérieuse. *NABU* 1994/3: 51-52.

Charpin, D. 2004. Chroniques bibliographiques 3. Données nouvelles sur la région du Petit Zab au XVIIIe siècle av. J.-C. *RA* 98: 151-178.

Dolce, R. 2004. The "Head of the Enemy" in the Sculptures from the Palaces of Nineveh: an Example of "Cultural Migration" ?. *Iraq* 46: 121-131.

Dolce, R. 2006. Têtes en guerre. In S. D'Onofrio and A. C. Taylor (eds), *La Guerre en Tête, Actes de la journée d'études "La guerre en tête" organisée par le Collège de France-LAS-CNRS, Université de Paris*

X, *Janvier 2003, Cahiers d'anthropologie sociale* 2: 33-46. Paris.

Dolce, R. 2014. Beyond Defeat. The Psychological Annihilation of the Vanquished in Pre-Classical Near Eastern Visual Communication. In H. Neumann *et alii* (eds), *Krieg und Frieden im Alten Vorderasien. 52e Rencontre Assyriologique Internationale.* International Congress of Assyriology and Near Eastern Archaeology, Münster, 17.–21. Juli 2006, AOAT 401: 237-267. Münster.

Dolce, R. 2016. Headless Mortals and Gods. Some Remarks on Decapitation in the Ancient Near East. R. A. Stucky *et alii* (eds), *Proceedings of the 9th International Congress of the Archaeology of the Ancient Near East (ICAANE),*Basel, *9-13 June 2014,*Vol.I: 83-97. Wiesbaden.

Donadoni, S. 1985. I nemici decapitati della tavolozza di Narmer. In M. Liverani *et alii* (eds), *Studi di Paletnologia in onore di Salvatore M. Puglisi*: 501-502. Roma.

Durand, J.-M. 1998. *Documents épistolaires du Palais de Mari*, vol. I. Paris.

Durand, J.-M. 2000. *Documents épistolaires du Palais de Mari*, vol. III. Paris.

Forest, J. D. 2009. Nouvelles réflexions sur Çatal Höyük. *Paléorient* 35: 113-115.

Gelb, I. J. 1973. Prisoners of War in Early Mesopotamia. *JNES* 32: 70-98.

Gerlach, J. 2000. Tradition-Adaption-Innovation: Zur Reliefkunst Nordsyriens/Südanatoliens in neuassyrischer Zeit. In G. Bunnens (ed), *Essays on Syria in the Iron Age*, ANES Suppl.7: 235-257. Louvain-Paris-Sterling, Virginia.

Glassner, J.-J. 2006. Couper des têtes en Mésopotamie. In S. D'Onofrio and A. C. Taylor (eds), *La Guerre en Tête, Actes de la journée d'études "La guerre en tête" organisée par le Collège de France-LAS-CNRS, Université de Paris X, Janvier 2003, Cahiers d'anthropologie sociale* 2: 47-55. Paris.

Grayson, A. K. 1976. *Assyrian Royal Inscriptions, vol.2, From Tiglath-pileser I to Ashur-nasir-apli II.* Wiesbaden.

Grayson, A. K. 1991. *Assyrian Rulers of the Early First Millenium BC (1114-859 BC), vol. I.* Toronto.

Harrison, T. P. 2005. The Neo-Assyrian Governor's Residence at Tell Ta'yinat. *BCSMS* 40: 23-32.

Hodder, I. 2009. An Archaeological Response. *Paléorient* 35: 109-111.

Jean, C.-F. 1950. *Lettres Diverses*, ARM II. Paris.

Jean, C. 2005. Des rapaces dévoreurs d'ennemis: un symbole de la victoire royale. In Ph. Talon and V. Ven Der Stede (eds), *Si un Homme… Textes offerts en hommage à André Finet,* Subartu XVI: 85-97. Turnhout.

Kaim, B. 2000. Killing and Dishonouring the Royal Statue in the Mesopotamian World. In S. Graziani (ed), *Studi sul Vicino Oriente Antico dedicati alla memoria di Luigi Cagni*, Napoli: 515-520.

Kaploni, P. 2002. The Bet Yerah Jar Inscription and the Annals of King Dewen-Dewen as "King Narmer Redivivus". In E. C. van den Brink and T. E. Lewy (eds), *Egypt and the Levant*: 464-486. London-New York.

Köhler, E.C. 2002. History or Ideology? New Reflections on the Narmer Palette and the Nature of Foreign Relations in Pre-and Early Dynastic Egypt. In E. C. Van den Brink and T. E. Lewy (eds), *Egypt and the Levant*: 499-513. London-New York.

Lafont, B. 1988. La correspondance d'Iddiyatum. In D. Charpin *et alii*, *Archives Epistolaires de Mari I/2*, ARM XXVI: 461-541. Paris.

Matthiae, P. 1995. Intarsi con aquile leontocefale e tori androcefali. In P. Matthiae *et alii* (eds), *Ebla. Alle origini della civiltà urbana*: 277-278. Milano.

Matthiae, P. 1998. *Ninive*. Milano.

May, N. N. 2010. Decapitation of Statues and Mutilation of the Image's Facial Features. In W. Horowitz *et alii* (eds), *A Woman of Valor: Jerusalem Ancient Near Eastern Studies in Honor of Joan Goodnick Westenholz*: 105-117. Madrid.

May N. N. (ed) 2012. *Iconoclasm and Text Destruction in the ANE and Beyond. The Oriental Institute Dedicates this Volume to the Memory of Eleanor Guralnick 1929-2012*, OIS 8. Chicago.

Mellaart, J. 1967. *Çatal Hüyük A Neolithic Town in Anatolia*. London.

Meuszyński, J. 1981. *Die Rekonstruktion der Reliefdarstellungen und ihrer Anordnung im Nordwestpalast von Kalhu (Nimrud)*. Mainz-am-Rhein.

Miglus, P. A. 2003. Die Siegesstele des Königs Daduša von Ešnunna und ihre Stellung in der Kunst Mesopotamiens und der Nachbargebiete. In R. Dittmann *et alii* (eds), *Altertumswissenschaften im Dialog Festschrift für Wolfram Nagel*: 397-420. Münster.

Miglus, P. A. 2008. Kings Go into Battle. Representations of the Mesopotamian Ruler as a Warrior. In Ph. Abrahami and L. Battini (eds), *Les armées du Proche-Orient ancient (IIIe-Ier mill.av.J.-C.)*, BAR International Series 1855: 231-246. Oxford, Archeopress.

Minunno, G. 2008a. La mutilation du corps de l'ennemi. In Ph. Abrahami and L. Battini (eds), *Les armées du Proche-Orient ancient (IIIe-Ier mill.av.J.-C.)*, BAR International Series 1855: 247-255. Oxford, Archeopress.

Minunno, G. 2008b. Pratiche di mutilazione dei nemici caduti nel Vicino Oriente antico. *Mesopotamia* 43: 9-29.

Moortgat, A. 1969. *The Art of Ancient Mesopotamia*. London-New York.

Nadali, D. 2001-2003. Guerra e morte: l'annullamento del nemico nella condizione di vinto. *Scienze dell'Antichità* 11: 51-70.

Nadali, D. 2007. Monuments of War, War of Monuments. Some Considerations on Commemorating War in the Third Millennium BC. *Or* 76: 336-367.

Nadali, D. 2008. La stele di Daduša come documento storico dell'età paleobabilonese. Immagini e iscrizione a confronto. *VO* 14: 129-146.

Nigro, L. 1997. Legittimazione e consenso: iconologia, religione e politica nelle stele di Sargon di Akkad. *CMAO* 7: 351-392.

Novotny, J. and Watanabe, C. E. 2008. After the Fall of Babylon: A New Look at the Presentation Scene on Assurbanipal Relief BM ME 124945-6. *Iraq* 70: 105-125.

Orthmann, W. 1971. *Untersuchungen zur Späthethitischen Kunst*. Bonn.

Richardson, S. 2007. Death and Dismemberment in Mesopotamia: Discorporation between the Body and Body Politic. *In* N. Laneri (ed), *Performing Death. Social Analysis of Funerary Traditions in the Ancient Near East and Mediterranean*, OIS 3: 189-208. Chicago, McNaughton & Gunn.

Talalay, L. E. 2004. Heady Business: Skulls, Heads and Decapitation in Neolithic Anatolia and Greece. *JMA* 17: 139-163.

Testart, A. 2008. Des crânes et des vautours *ou* la guerre oubliée. *Paléorient* 34: 33-58. Paris.

Thureau-Dangin, F. - Dunand, M. 1936. *Til Barsip (2 vols.)*. Paris.

Watanabe, C. E. 2004. The "Continuous Style" in the Narrative Schemes of Aüüssurbanipal's Reliefs. *Iraq* 46: 103-114. London

Watanabe, C. E. 2008. A Compositional Analysis of the Battle of Til-Tuba. In H. Kühne *et alii* (eds), *Proceedings of 4th International Congress of the Archaeology of the Ancient Near East (ICAANE), Berlin , 29 March-3 April 2004, Freie Universität Berlin*, Vol.1: 601-612. Wiesbaden.

Welton, L. *et alii* 2011. Tell Tayinat in the Late Third Millenium. Recent Investigations of the Tayinat Archaeological Project, 2008-2010. *Anatolica* 37: 147-185.

Wiggermann, F. A. 1992. *Mesopotamian Protective Spirits. The Ritual Texts*. Gröningen.

Winter, I. J. 1985. After the Battle is Over: The Stele of the Vultures and the Beginning of Historical Narrative Art in the Art of the Ancient Near East. In H. L. Kessler and M. Shreve Simpson (eds), *Pictorial Narrative in Antiquity and the Middle Ages*, Studies in the History of Art 16): 11-32. Washington.

Woolley, L. and Barnett, R. D. 1952. *Carchemish. Part III. Report on the Excavations at Jerablus on behalf of the British Museum*. London.

Abstract

In current usage, the expression "losing one's head" describes various states in which an individual may find himself or herself after a traumatic event of some sort, physical or psychological, from anger to pain to falling in love and so forth. The expression is thus transposed from its primary meaning, referring to a concrete condition of extreme crudeness, to other meanings relating to the temporary or even permanent lack of mental faculties, alienation, but with a common denominator that we could sum up as a loss of "self-control".

This premise is the starting point for some general and analytical reflections on the significance of decapitation in times of war for those who perpetrate it and those who suffer it, in the light of the visual communications of Mesopotamia and Syria between the III and I mill. BC. Here this procedure played a special role, which in my opinion cannot be compared to others, corresponding to a different level of alienation/disability on the part of the defeated, in fact and meaning.

Some recurrent features of the figurative cultures of the ANE, constants in the representation of beheading and related practices before and after the act in images and writing, become extremely long-lasting narrative codes; exemplary evidence of this is provided by the Spanish tapestries of the XVI c. AD with the stories of Judith and Holofernes.

My objective was thus to document this issue in a trans-chronological perspective aiming to highlight some conditions, relations and values surrounding this specific act in times of war. The severed head is always a "desired object" and is often the object of attention of several living subjects who interact in its various later destinations.

The analysis starts from the selection of some figurative codes and their various associations in the numerous works considered where the SH is the focus, surveying the evidence from the prehistoric to the Neo-Assyrian period in Anatolia, Syria and Mesopotamia. Supported by the textual data where relevant, I suggest iconographic and ideological interpretations that often differ from those hitherto advanced.

Key words:

DECAPITATION - WAR - VISUAL COMMUNICATION - MESOPOTAMIA - SYRIA - III-I MILL. BC

Where is the Public?
A New Look at the Brutality Scenes in Neo-Assyrian Royal Inscriptions and Art

Ariel Bagg*

"Of course, if we use the word propaganda our first question must be:
'Where is the public'?"
(B. Landsberger 1989: 41)

Introduction[1]

"The Assyrians were not only brutal, but they were proud of being brutal". These words are taken from the inaugural lecture to the 39th *Rencontre Assyriologique*, which took place in Heidelberg in 1992 and dealt with Assyrian history. With his characteristic combination of scholarship and fine irony, Winfried Lambert pointed to a common, deeply anchored *topos* concerning the Assyrians which influenced Assyriology and neighbouring disciplines for a long time. Even if in the last twenty years valuable studies have clearly shown the diversity of the Assyrian culture, a whiff of their image as the musclemen of Mesopotamian history in contrast to the wise Sumerians and Babylonians still persists. They are characterized as especially brutal, terrorizing their enemies and bullying them by means of propagandistic inscriptions and depictions. An especially important argument is the fact that they described in detail the atrocities they committed[2] and depicted them with a terrifying realism.[3] The question I want to deal with in this study is, if a propagandistic purpose can be attributed to the depictions of atrocities in Assyrian iconography, as is commonly accepted. If royal inscriptions and palace reliefs are interpreted as a message, and even a propagandistic one, sent by the king, the central question is that after the intended audience. In other words, as Benno Landsberger pointedly asked: "Where is the public?".[4] As the question is relevant for both written and iconographic sources, and the narrative palace reliefs are indeed royal inscriptions in pictures,[5] I will analyse first the cruelties attested in the texts and then those depicted on the slabs that covered the walls of the Assyrian palaces.

At this point let me make some methodological comments. First, I will focus on the Neo-Assyrian period. Second, the subject of this study is the description and representation of the committed atrocities, and not the atrocities themselves.[6] Third, I will consider only the acts of cruelty committed after a battle or siege, namely when the hostilities had ceased and the enemy was already defeated, and not those perpetrated during the combat. It is not necessary to say that every war, past or present, is cruel. Close combat with cut weapons as practiced in Assyrian times was brutal, but this was at that time an immanent feature of warfare, which could not be executed in any other way. Finally, while we have a large corpus of royal inscriptions covering all of the Neo-Assyrian period, the iconographical material is highly fragmentary. As Neo-Assyrian palaces have only partially been excavated, in some cases to a very small extent, we know only a minor part of the wall reliefs. Furthermore, a great part of the slabs is fragmentarily preserved, and the sources are not homogeneously distributed along the period under study. However, the available corpus can be considered representative, allowing general remarks, but without forgetting the mentioned restrictions.

Before dealing with the sources, some brief remarks concerning the alleged "Assyrian brutality" are necessary. Of course, it is not my aim to justify or minimize the acts of brutality committed by the Assyrian soldiers and officers, but rather to set them in their historical context. Were the Assyrians brutal? Clearly, yes. Were the Assyrians as brutal as they presented themselves in the written and iconographical sources? The answer is no, they were more brutal, because we do not know all the details, and the reality must have surpassed by far the descriptions in words or the depictions. Even if both are impressive, they lack in detail and realism; we do not hear the screams of the victims or the crying of those who attended the executions, we do not see the blood flowing from the bodies or from the hands of the

---

* University of Heidelberg, Seminar für Sprachen und Kulturen des Vorderen Orients.

[1] I am much indebted to Dr. Brigitte Finkbeiner for reviewing my English.
[2] "The account was probably intended not only to describe what happened, but also to frighten anyone who might dare to resist" (referring to Ashurnasirpal's II inscriptions), Bleibtreu 1991: 57.
[3] "In order to dissuade disloyalty and rebellion by foreigners and courtiers (Russell 1991: 256), the artists displayed the atrocities incurred by the enemy with rather macabre realism", Reed 2007: 106.
[4] Landsberger 1989: 41.
[5] Villard 1988: 422.

[6] This subject was recently treated by Fuchs in an excellent article (Fuchs 2009).

Assyrian executioners, we do not smell the stink of blood and dismembered bodies.

Were the Assyrians more brutal than other peoples in the Ancient Near East? No. At that time war was carried out by all in the same way, and brutality is largely attested from the third millennium to the Persians, who used impaling among other ways of execution.[7] Soldiers carrying severed heads are depicted in the Ebla Standard,[8] and the Hebrew Bible mentions plenty of atrocities[9]. The Assyrians were only more successful than their enemies and had therefore more opportunities to act violently because they were militarily superior. Assyrian soldiers were killed in the battlefield in the same way as their adversaries and we can only guess what happened to Assyrians when they were captured by an enemy thirsty for revenge.

Were the Assyrians especially brutal in the context of human history? The answer is again no. A survey of brutal acts committed since the Assyrians up to the present would be a huge work going beyond the scope of this study. However, the mention of the Inquisition, the Conquest of America or the Holocaust suffices – by the ways in which civilians were pursued, denigrated and murdered as well as by the dimension of the casualties (up to many millions!) – to make it clear that to credit the Assyrians with a specially brutal character does not correspond to the historical facts. Moreover, they would probably not even be among the top-ten in a ranking of human brutality. Lamentably, brutality is one of the features which distinguish humans from animals, as there exists no other living creature capable of such cruel acts as humans are. Therefore, I think it is time to finish speaking of "Assyrian brutality".

Catalogue of atrocities: The written sources

The historical accounts of the Assyrian royal inscriptions contain more or less detailed reports of the king's military campaigns on which our reconstruction of the political history of Assyria is based. In some cases the scribes did not limit themselves to mentioning that a certain city was conquered, but gave details about how it was done and what happened after the conquest. On the basis of these passages it is possible to draw up a catalogue of twenty-two atrocities (*Figure 6.1*) in connection with three different groups, all of them related to the enemy: soldiers, members of the elite and civilians. I have considered as "atrocities" on the one hand, acts of brute physical force against living prisoners – in most cases painful executions and in others brutal humiliations – and on the other hand, the brutal treatment of dead bodies or parts of them. As mentioned above, only acts committed after the combats were taken into account. Deportations

were not included in the catalogue, as, even if they were traumatic, people stayed alive and were able to begin a new life in another part of the empire where they were integrated in the course of one or two generations.

The catalogue of atrocities comprises the following types:

Group A: Soldiers

1. To fill a river or a gorge with the bodies of fallen soldiers, in some cases probably still alive
2. To heap the bodies of fallen soldiers (dead or still alive) before a city or in the battlefield
3. To erect towers of heads before a conquered city
4. To hang heads on trees on a mountain or in the courtyard of the beaten enemy's palace (only Anp II)
5. To spread out soldiers alive on the enemy's palace walls (only Anp II)
6. To gouge out survivors' eyes after a battle (only Anp II)
7. To cut hands, arms, lips, ears or noses of living soldiers[10]
8. To burn alive (only Anp II)
9. To impale, in some cases explicitly alive

Four further *topoi*, which often appear in the royal inscriptions, are rather the natural consequences of a combat with cut weapons than atrocities committed after the battle, so that they are not included in the catalogue. They create a dramatic effect and stress the magnitude of the power of the Assyrian army and its king:

A. To let the soldiers' blood flow into a river or gorge[11]
B. To dye a mountain or river red with the soldiers' blood[12]
C. To fill the streets of a city with killed soldiers[13]
D. To dye the streets and houses of a city red with the blood of killed soldiers[14]

Group B: Members of the elite

10. To impale, in some cases explicitly alive
11. To flay alive and eventually drape the skin over the wall of the enemy's city

[7] Jacobs 2009.

[8] Dolce 2004: 124–126.

[9] For instance Joshuas's conquest of Ai (Jos 8: 25–28) or Hazor (Jos 11: 10-14) where everyone was put to the sword.

[10] Sennacherib did not cut the testicles of his enemies as quoted by Bleibtreu 1991: 60, who used an outdated translation. According to RINAP 3/1, Nr. 22, iv, 10–11 he cut the lips (*sapsapāte*) of his Elamite enemies.

[11] RIMA 3: 103.1, iv, 28–29 (Šamšī-Adad V); TCL 3: 135 (Sargon II); RINAP 4: Nr. 1, v, 14 (Esarhaddon); BIWA: 226, F, ii, 65–66 (Ashurbanipal).

[12] RIMA 2: 101.1, I, 53; RIMA 2: ii, 17–18. 114; RIMA 2: 010.19, 81 (Ashurnasirpal II); RIMA 3: 102.1, 61'; RIMA 3: 102.2, ii, 50. 73; RIMA 3: iii, 1–2 (Shalmaneser III); RINAP 1: Tigl 20, 3'–4'; RINAP 1: Tigl 47, 48 (Tiglath-Pileser III); TCL 3: 135 (Sargon II); BIWA: 226, F, ii, 63 (Ashurbanipal).

[13] RIMA 2: 101.1, ii, 55 (Ashurnasirpal II); RINAP 3/2: Nr. 223, 45–46 (Sennacherib).

[14] RIMA 2: 101.1, ii, 55–56 (Ashurnasirpal II); RIMA 3: 102.1, iii, 11–13 (Šamšī-Adad V).

No	Type of Atrocity	Ašd2	Anp	Slm	Ša5	Tigl	Sg	Sn	Ash	Asb
Group A: Soldiers										
1	To fill a river with corpses of soldiers		x[1]	x[2]	x[3]	x[4]		x[5]		x[6]
2	To heap the bodies (dead or still alive)		x[7]	x[8]	x[9]		x[10]		x[11]	
3	To erect towers of heads		x[12]	x[13]					x[14]	
4	To hang heads on trees		x[15]							
5	To spread out alive		x[16]							
6	To gouge out the eyes after a battle		x[17]							
7	To mutilate		x[18]			x[19]		x[20]		x[21]
8	To burn alive		x[22]							
9	To impale (alive)		x[23]	x[24]		x[25]		x[26]	x[27]	
Group B: Members of the elite										
10	To impale (alive)		x[28]			x[29]		x[30]		
11	To flay alive (and drape the skin over wall)	x[31]	x[32]				x[33]	x[34]		x[35]
12	To hang a head on the neck							x[36]		x[37]
13	To let grind the bones of the ancestors									x[38]
14	To expose in chains with ring and rope							x[39]		x[40]
15	To pull out the tongue									x[41]
16	To behead and expose the head (Te'umman)									x[42]
17	To slaughter like a sheep (to eviscerate)									x[43]
18	To dismember									x[44]
Group C: Civilian population										
19	To burn adolescent boys and girls		x[45]							
20	To execute and dismember					x[46]			x[47]	x[48]
21	To impale									x[49]
22	To flay alive									x[50]

FIGURE 6.1: ATROCITIES IN NEO-ASSYRIAN ROYAL INSCRIPTIONS

1 RIMA 2, 101.1, i, 53; id., ii, 17–18; id., ii, 41–42; id., ii, 115; RIMA 2, 101.19, 81–82.
2 RIMA 3, 102.1, 59'–60'; RIMA 3, 102.2, i, 39; id., ii, 98–102; RIMA 3, 102.14, 146; id., 102.28, 33. 44.
3 RIMA 3, 103.1, iii, 40–41.
4 RINAP 1, Tigl 9, 7'.
5 RINAP 3/1, Nr. 22, vi, 9–10.
6 BIWA 222, B, v, 97–99; id 226, F, ii, 64; AfO 8, 185, 35.
7 RIMA 2, 101.1, i, 109. 118; id., ii, 108; RIMA 2, 101.19, 75.
8 RIMA 3, 102.28, 34.
9 RIMA 2, 103.1, iv, 30.
10 Fuchs Sg, Stier, 33–34.
11 RINAP 4, Nr. 1, iv, 70.
12 RIMA 2, 101.1, i, 64. 116; id., ii, 18–19. 107–109; id., iii, 106–107; RIMA 2, 101.19, 74–76.
13 RIMA 3, 102.1, 16. 32. 62'; RIMA 3, 102.2, i, 34–35; id., ii, 53. 73.
14 RINAP 4, Nr. 33, Tablet 2, ii, 10.
15 RIMA 2, 101.1, i, 118; id., ii, 43. 71–72.
16 RIMA 2, 101.1, ii, 72.
17 RIMA 2, 101.1, i, 116; id., iii, 113.
18 RIMA 2, 101.1, i, 116; id., ii, 15; RIMA 2, 101.19, 82.
19 RINAP 1, Tigl 7, 7.
20 RINAP 3/1, Nr. 22, vi, 11–12; RINAP 3/2, Nr. 230, 93. The soldiers mutilated by Sennacherib were later flayed by Ashurbaniapal (BIWA 236, C, IX, 56'–66'.
21 BIWA 237, F, iii, 49–52.
22 RIMA 2, 101.1, i, 108. 116; id., ii, 108; RIMA 2, 101.19, 75.
23 RIMA 2, 101.1, i, 28–29; id., ii, 109; RIMA 2, 101.19, 76; in the following cases soldiers were impaled alive: RIMA 2, 101.1, iii, 33. 84. 108. 112.
24 RIMA 3, 102.14, 154.
25 RINAP 1, Tigl 7, 7; id., Nr. 8, 5.

26 RINAP 3/1, Nr. 22, i, 59–60.
27 RINAP 4, Nr. 33, Tablet 2, ii, 11.
28 RIMA 2, 101.1, i, 89–92.
29 RINAP 1, Tigl 20, 9'–10' (alive); id., Tigl. 39, 9–10.
30 In this case the corpes were hung on towers: RINAP 3/1, Nr. 22, iii, 9–10; id., Nr. 23, iii, 9.
31 RIMA 2, 98.1, 39–41.
32 RIMA 2, 101.1, i, 89–92. 93. 110.
33 Fuchs Sg, Ann, 83; id., Prunk 35. 49.
34 RINAP 3/1, Nr. 17, iv, 82–86.
35 BIWA 228, B, vi, 83–87: 87–88; BIWA 249, A, x, 5; AfO 8, 185, 28; id., 195, 59. 60; Streck Asb, 317–318 (η).
36 RINAP 4, Nr. 1, iii, 32–38.
37 BIWA 227, B, vi, 50–51; id., C, vii, 49–50; BIWA 243, A, vii, 45–50.
38 BIWA 228, B, vi, 93 – vii, 2; id 241, F, v, 49–54.
39 RINAP 4, Nr. 1, iii, 39–42.
40 BIWA 246, A, viii, 8–13. 27–28; id 249, A, ix, 107–111; AfO 8, 183, 26.
41 BIWA 228, B, vi, 83–87.
42 BIWA 225, B, vi, 1–3; id 230, B, vii, 60–61; id 227, B, vi, 50–51. 62–62. 66–69; AfO 8, 181, 9–10. 11.12.14; AfO 8, 201, 72; Streck Asb, 312-313 (γ).
43 BIWA 228, B, vi, 87–89; id., 303–304, Nr. 29; vgl. SAA 2, 6, § 70.
44 BIWA 231, C, ix, 42–44.
45 RIMA 2, 101.1, i, 19; id., ii, 1. 17–18. 43. 109–110; RIMA 2, 101.19, 77.
46 RINAP 1, Tigl 19, 2–3.
47 RINAP 4, Nr. 33, Tablet 2, iii, 23'–24'.
48 BIWA 231, C, ix, 42–44; id 235, A iv, 70–73.
49 BIWA 214, B, i, 95 – ii, 2; id 249, A, ix, 123–124; WO 7, 85, v, 1.
50 BIWA 214, B, i, 95 – ii, 2; id. C, ii, 130 – iii, 5; BIWA 231, C, ix, 42–44.

12. To hang the head of a rebel on the neck of an elite member (even relatives)
13. To let grind the bones of the ancestors (only Asb)
14. To expose rebels in chains with a pierced ring and a rope, sometimes together with animals
15. To pull out the tongue (only Asb)
16. To mutilate a corpse (beheading) or part of it (Teumman's head)
17. To slaughter like a sheep, namely to eviscerate (only Asb)
18. To dismember after execution (only Asb)

Group C: Civilians

19. To burn adolescent boys and girls (only Anp II)
20. To execute and dismember
21. To impale (only Asb)
22. To flay alive (only Asb)[15]

To discuss each of these atrocities in detail is out of the scope of this study, but some general remarks are possible.[16] Horrible and sanguinary as this catalogue may be, it must first be taken into account that not all atrocities were committed by every king. In the case of the nine cruelties committed against soldiers, four are attested only in Ashurnasirpal's II inscriptions (types 4, 5, 6, and 8). In the case of the elite members, also nine atrocities, five were committed only by Ashurbanipal (types 13, 15, 17, and 18).[17] When we look at the third group, the civilians, from the four acts of cruelty, one goes to the account of Ashurnasirpal II, and two others to that of Ashurbanipal. Considering the whole Neo-Assyrian period and the different types of brutal acts perpetrated by each king, two kings stand clearly out: Ashurbanipal with 13 types and Ashurnasirpal II with 12; they are followed at a distance by Tiglath-pileser III, Sennacherib, and Esarhaddon with half of those figures (5, 5, and 6 respectively). Furthermore, the contextual analysis of the atrocities clearly shows that they were neither carried out always, namely in the great majority of the cases, nor were they aleatory acts. The exercise of brutality was a structural element of Assyrian domination policy: brutal acts were committed in selected cases to make clear the rules and to discourage potential rebellions. The Assyrian domination policy was pragmatic and success-oriented: selective dissuasion by means of terror limited the costs

and perils of further insurrections, and at the same time further bloodshed.

Another remarkable feature is the fact that civilians were seldom the object of brutalities. The burning of young people is only attested in Ashurnasirpal's II inscriptions, impaling and flaying of civilians were only implemented by Ashurbanipal, who also carried out mutilations, which were otherwise only perpetrated by Tiglath-pileser III and Esarhaddon. Therefore, among the selective use of brutal punishments, the acts against the civilian population were not the rule, but a seldom case. If the Assyrians had committed such cruelties against civilians more often or as a usual procedure, they would not have omitted to mention that in their inscriptions, probably with one exception. It is curious that no case of rape is attested, considering that the rape of women after the conquest of a city was a widely-used procedure up to the Second World War and is not even completely eradicated in the present.[18] As it is improbable that the Assyrian soldiers, after a long siege or battle, entered into a city looting, burning and destroying but not touching a single woman: why is that not mentioned?[19] According to A. Fuchs, rape was on the one hand no heroic deed for the Assyrians, and on the other hand it was an unauthorized act perpetrated by soldiers who had gone out of the king's control.[20] As the king presented himself as having the total control of the empire and the army, an independent and shameful act by the soldiers must not be included in the accounts.

Summing up: Brutality was applied in a deliberate and selective way to discourage potential insurrections or resistance to the Assyrian rule, but had the description and depiction of the brutalities the same purpose?

The audience of the royal inscriptions

In answer to the question about the public of the royal inscriptions two aspects must be considered: 1) the intended and potential audience, and 2) the context of the inscriptions, namely their location. Furthermore, we must consider three levels in the reception of the message: a text could be seen (without being read), it could be read, or it could be listened to during a reading.

The intended audience is related to the text, where it can be implied or explicitly mentioned (*Figure 6.2*). Some texts mention the future kings explicitly and warn them not to destroy the inscriptions. The implied addressees of the inscriptions were the gods, especially Assur, for whose glory the king performed his deeds. The potential audience was a function of a) the accessibility

---

[15] A further way of execution, namely to rip out the heart of a prisoner, is rarely attested. A fragmentary administrative text mentions prisoners of unknown status "(with) their hearts ripped out (and) their tongues torn out, and *mutilated*", SAA 7: 144, i, 2'–5'. The same way of execution may be alluded to in a fragmentary caption included in a collection of captions dating from the reign of Ashurbanipal, BIWA: 311, 58, ii, 3' (AfO 8: 195, Nr. 58, ii, 3), see Fuchs 2009: 73, footnote 13.

[16] For a comprehensive study see Fuchs 2009; for a compact account of corpse abuse in the Middle- and Neo-Assyrian periods see Richardson 2007: 196–200.

[17] I am referring here to the written evidence, which I consider representative for the present study. Of course it cannot be ruled out that the same brutalities were committed by other kings.

[18] Rape is punished in the Middle-Assyrian laws, Roth 1997: 174–175, tablet A, § 55. Furthermore, the rape of the women of perjured vassals is mentioned among the curses in Esarhaddon's succession treaty, SAA 2: 428–429.

[19] A possible depiction of a rape during a military campaign against the Arabs is discussed below.

[20] Fuchs 2009: 71–72.

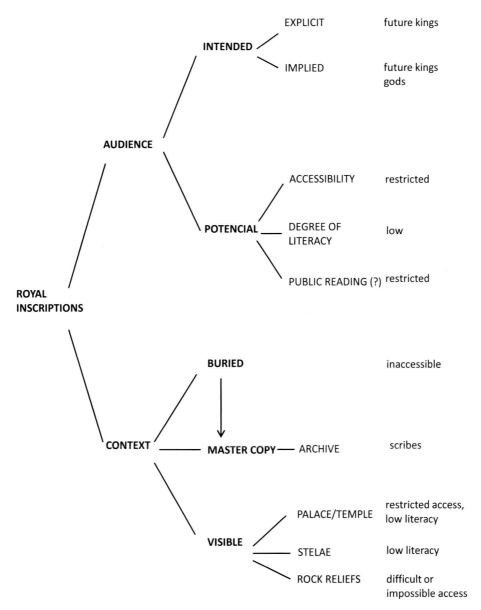

FIGURE 6.2: THE ADDRESSEES OF THE ROYAL INSCRIPTIONS.

of the inscriptions, namely of the rooms were they were displayed, b) the degree of literacy, and c) the possibility to attend a public reading. The accessibility to the different rooms was more or less restricted, from the more private areas to the more public ones of the palace, as we will see when analysing the audience of the reliefs. To get access to a certain room did not mean to understand an inscription, as even in the most optimistic case, very few people were able to read a cuneiform text written in standard Babylonian. This circle was restricted to the scribes and scholars. It is possible that part of the population was able to write and read Neo-Assyrian, but it was an occupational capability restricted to a certain number of signs used in letters and economic documents. The great part of the native population and all foreigners (leaving aside some diplomats and interpreters) were not able to read them. Furthermore enough time and sufficient lighting were needed.

The public reading of a royal inscription was postulated by A. Leo Oppenheim based on his interpretation of Sargon's report about his eighth campaign against Urartu in 714 BC.[21] This text pertains to a reduced group of royal reports written as a letter to the god Assur.[22] The fact that Sargon mentions in the introductory passage not only the god Assur, but the gods, the inhabitants and the palace of the city of Assur[23] induced Oppenheim to postulate that this kind of accounts were intended to be read in public after each military campaign,[24] and not (only) to

---

[21] Oppenheim 1960.
[22] The group includes a fragmentary letter of Shalmaneser IV (RIMA 3: 105.3), Sargon's II report about his campaign against Urartu in 714 (TCL 3), Esarhaddon's report about his campaign against Šubria (RINAP 4: Nr. 33) and Ashurbanipal's letters referring to his military campaigns against the Arabs (BIWA: 76–82 and Weippert 1973-74: 74–85) and to the war against Elam (Bauer 1933: 83–84).
[23] TCL 3: 1-5.
[24] Oppenheim 1960: 143–147 (especially 143).

be deposited in the temple, as is mentioned in the text's colophon.[25] Leaving aside that the population of a city is only mentioned in this text, it must be considered that this kind of letters were part of a communication process between the king and the god Assur. They were rather intended to be read before the statue of the god than in front of the public.[26] It is unknown whether Sargon's report was ever read in public. I take it that a reading of some royal inscriptions before the king and his entourage is plausible, especially in times of inner political trouble, but a public reading before foreigners, who were not able to understand, is less probable.

When we consider the context of the inscriptions, we realize that most of them were buried, making them inaccessible for the contemporaries. Only the gods and the later kings, when they found the inscriptions during restoration or building works, were able to get the message. This limits the access to the written message to the master copies for the buried inscriptions and to the displayed inscriptions. In the former case only the palace scribes come into consideration. The possibility to read those inscriptions which were visible in the palaces and temples was highly restricted by the degree of accessibility to the rooms and by the degree of literacy, as mentioned above. Inscriptions on stelae and rock reliefs in foreign territories will hardly have been read because of the different languages and writing systems. Furthermore, some inscriptions accompanying rock reliefs were inaccessible or not easily accessible for human eyes, like Sennacherib's Bavian Inscription, chiselled three times in a mountain gorge but out of reach for mortals.

At a verbal level, the royal inscriptions, specially the narrative accounts, were intended for the gods and the future rulers, probably at least in some cases also for the elite as a kind of self-indoctrination. At a non-verbal level, the inscriptions expressed the greatness of a king, who controlled the use of script and was able to have such texts written. In the case of the stelae and rock reliefs in foreign regions, they functioned at a non-verbal level to make clear the rules of the game: "We were here and we will come back if you do not observe the rules". Considering that the main audience were the gods and future rulers, and that for others the inscriptions worked on a non-verbal level, it is not correct to speak of propaganda: there was neither a public for it nor was propaganda their main goal. Of course the inscriptions were biased, but what else can be expected from inscriptions written by a ruler for his own glorification? Which king in the history or ruler in the present mentions in official texts or speeches errors, defeats or casualties?

And now we arrive at the description of cruelties committed against enemies which rebelled against the king. The proper punishment of rebels was part of the war: the king punished the enemies of Assyria, protected their citizens, and had the control over life and death. The descriptions of what we perceive as brutalities were only part of the facts and of the story, like the descriptions of the sieges, the battles or the tribute received. They were not perceived as brutalities by the Assyrians and had no propagandistic goal, as there was no public. The acts themselves were an instrument for intimidation, but not their descriptions. What about the brutality scenes?

Catalogue of atrocities: The iconographic sources

Turning to the iconographical material, the main sources are the reliefs carved on the stone plates which decorated the palace walls in Kalḫu, Dūr-Šarrukēn and Nineveh, the bronze bands which covered temple and palace gates in the city of Imgur-Illil (Balawat), and the wall paintings from the Assyrian palace in Til-Barsip. As mentioned above, we have only a minor part of the once existing reliefs, and the material is unequally distributed among the different Assyrian kings. If we have a relative large number of reliefs dating from the reigns of Sennacherib and Ashurbanipal, their quantity and state of preservation decrease noticeably in the case of Sargon. From the reliefs of Shalmaneser, Tiglath-pileser and Esarhaddon very little or nothing at all is preserved. Ashurnasirpal's narrative reliefs are again relatively few and his wonderful bronze bands are only fragmentarily preserved.[27] However, the analysis of the available material shows interesting results concerning brutality scenes.

The catalogue includes 56 brutality scenes related to soldiers, members of the elite and civilians covering a spectrum of twelve different types (see catalogue in the Appendix):[28]

Group A: Soldiers

1. To fill a river with corpses, in some cases probably still alive, *Figure 6.3*[29]
2. To erect towers of heads before a city (only Slm), *Figure 6.4e*
3. To make a pile of heads for inventory, *Figures 6.5-6*

Group B: Elite Members

4. To impale, in some cases most probably alive, *Figures 6.4a, b, c* and *6.7*

---

[25] TCL 3: 426-430.
[26] After Pongratz-Leisten 1999: 273–274.

[27] Curtis and Talin 2008.
[28] The list takes up the 22 types attested in the royal inscriptions, with three additional types 23–25.
[29] The Assyrian soldier who appears in all the figures is on the same scale as the depicted scenes (with the exception of *Figure 6.4*) in order to show their relation to human scale. In *Figure 6.4* the soldier is on the same scale as the gates; the scenes are shown on a much greater scale.

FIGURE 6.3: BATTLE OF TIL-TUBA. A SOLDIER HOLDS TEUMMAN'S CUT-OFF HEAD (SECOND REGISTER FROM THE BOTTOM, LEFT SIDE; CAT.-NO 44); CORPSES OF DEFEATED ELAMITES ARE THROWN INTO THE RIVER ULAI (LOWER HALF, RIGHT SIDE; CAT.-NO 45). FROM BARNETT, BLEIBTREU AND TURNER 1998: PL. 296.

5. To flay alive, *Figures 6.8-9*
6. To let grind the bones of the ancestors (only Asb), *Figure 6.6*
7. To pull out the tongue (only Asb), *Figure 6.9*
8. To expose rebels with ring and rope, *Figure 6.10*
9. To execute by a cut in the throat and to behead, *Figures 6.4a*, *6.6* and *6.9*
10. To dismember, *Figure 6.4a*
11. To gouge out the eyes (only Sg), *Figure 6.11*

Group C: Civilians

12. To rape a woman (?) or to slit a pregnant woman's womb (?)[30] (only Asb)

A view at the distribution of the scenes (*Figure 6.12*) shows a high concentration of brutality scenes in Ashurbanipal's (19 out of 54), Sargon's (12 out of 54) and Sennacherib's (9 out of 54) reliefs. Considering the different types of cruelties depicted, again Ashurbanipal comes in first with 7 out of 12 types, followed at a distance by Sargon (6 out of 12), and Shalmaneser, Tiglath-pileser, Sargon and Sennacherib, each with 3 out of 12 types. The most cherished motive was that of severed heads brought for inventory, which is attested 17 times, followed by the filling of a river with corpses and the depiction of beheaded corpses or severed heads, each with 14 attestations, and impalements with 6 cases.

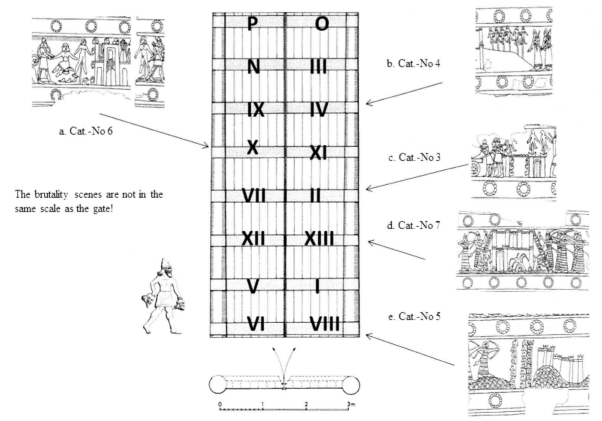

The brutality scenes are not in the same scale as the gate!

FIGURE 6.4: SHALMANESER'S BALAWAT GATES AS DISPLAYED IN THE BRITISH MUSEUM (CAT.-NOS 3–7). DOOR RECONSTRUCTION BASED ON SCHACHNER 2007: 24, FIG. 6; DEPICTIONS FROM SCHACHNER 2007: PLATES 2, 4, 8, 10 AND 13.

---

[30] See footnote 34.

FIGURE 6.5: SOLDIERS CARRYING SEVERED HEADS FOR INVENTORY (CAT.-NO 37). FROM BARNETT, BLEIBTREU AND TURNER 1998: PL. 210.

FIGURE 6.6: GRINDING THE ANCESTOR'S BONES (UPPER REGISTER, LEFT SIDE; CAT.-NO 40); SOLDIERS CARRYING SEVERED HEADS FOR INVENTORY (SECOND REGISTER FROM THE TOP, RIGHT SIDE; CAT.-NO 41); A SOLDIER HOLDS TEUMMAN'S CUT-OFF HEAD (SECOND REGISTER FROM THE TOP, LEFT SIDE; CAT.-NO 42). FROM BARNETT, BLEIBTREU AND TURNER 1998: PL. 288.

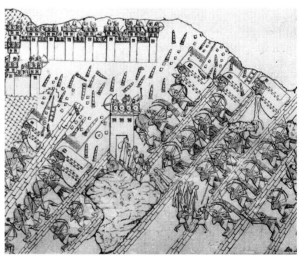

FIGURE 6.7: SIEGE OF LACHISH, IMPALEMENT OF THREE PRISONERS (CAT.-NO 30). FROM BARNETT, BLEIBTREU AND TURNER 1998: PL. 330.

Especially important for our purpose is the fact that the greatest variety of ways of execution (impalement, flaying, beheading, dismembering, gouging) or humiliations (grinding the bones of the ancestors, being exposed with ring and rope) concerns the second group, namely the members of the elite.

The analysis of the six impalement scenes allows some interesting observations. The texts mention that living persons as well as dead bodies could be impaled, and there is a great difference between being impaled dead or alive. Whereas for an already executed victim it is of no importance what happens to his dead body as he does not feel the pain anymore, to be impaled alive is a terrible way of being executed. Also in this case there are great differences. There are two ways of impaling, both intensely used in the Middle-Ages and shown in the Assyrian reliefs. The soft version was to drive a pointed stake into the victim's chest producing an almost immediate decease as vital organs were injured. This way is shown in three impalements depicted on Tiglath-pileser's, Sargon's and Sennacherib's reliefs (Cat.-Nos 8, 14 and 30). The other way consisted in introducing a pointed but slightly rounded stake into the lower end of the digestive tract of the victim and then bringing the stake into a vertical position, causing a slow and painful death. The three depictions of impalement on Shalmaneser's bronze bands undoubtedly show this version (Cat.-Nos 3, 4 and 6).

Another relevant point is the fact that most of the six depictions show just few impaled people: two, three or six persons in the case of Shalmaneser, three in the cases of Tiglath-pileser and Sennacherib, and exceptionally 14 in Sargon's reliefs (Cat.-No 15).[31] This agrees with the information of the written sources, namely that mainly members of the elite were executed in such a way,[32] whereas the impalement of civilians is only

---

[31] Conquest of Ḫarḫar (caption) in 716.
[32] For the impaled prisoners in Sennacherib's depiction of the conquest of Lachish see Ussishkin 2003.

FIGURE 6.8: FLAYING OF TWO PRISONERS (CAT.-NO 29). FROM BARNETT, BLEIBTREU AND TURNER 1998: PL. 338.

FIGURE 6.9: SOLDIERS FLAY PRISONERS WHILE ANOTHER ONE HOLDS A SEVERED HEAD (SECOND REGISTER FROM THE TOP; CAT.-NO 46); SOLDIERS PULL OUT THE TONGUE OF PRISONERS (THIRD REGISTER FROM THE TOP; CAT.-NO 47). FROM BARNETT, BLEIBTREU AND TURNER 1998: PL. 300.

attested in Ashurbanipal's inscriptions.[33] Leaving open the possibility that some of the impaled people in Sargon's depiction of the conquest of Ḫarḫar may have been civilians, there is only one depiction where a brutal act against the civilian population is shown, if the interpretation is correct: it is the possible depiction of the rape of a woman during one of Ashurbanipal's campaigns against Arab tribes (Cat.-No 54). This would be the only attestation for such a crime in the Assyrian sources.[34]

A last remark concerns a singular fact: In Ashurnasirpal's preserved narrative reliefs there is only one brutality scene (Cat.-No 1). Soldiers are shown carrying severed heads and even playing with them[35] while a bird holds another head in its claws. In his bronze bands there is also only one depiction of a beheaded body (Cat.-No 2). Taken into account the great variety and quantity of brutalities attested in Ashurnarsirpal's inscriptions, it is striking that no further cruelties are shown in the preserved material. In order to discuss the alleged intentionality and effect of these scenes, terrible as they undoubtedly are, it is necessary to consider them in their context, as they were mainly only details in greater compositions. Before doing that let me ask again the decisive question: where is the public?

The audience of the palace reliefs

In order to analyse who could have seen the depicted brutality scenes we must consider, as in the case of the royal inscriptions, two main aspects: on the one hand the intended and potential audience, and on the other hand the context of the iconographic sources (*Figure 6.13*).[36] We have no explicit indication about the intended audience, but considering that palace reliefs and reliefs on bronze bands contained the same message as the texts, we can say that the implied audience was primarily the future kings and the gods. A great difference between the written and the visual message is the circumstance that in the first case a special qualification is needed, namely the capability to read and understand, whereas

---

[33] Campaign to the West in 645 (Akkû) and first Egyptian campaign.

[34] I follow here the interpretation from SAA 2: 47, caption to fig. 13. Dubowsky 2009 (especially 412–418) proposes an alternative interpretation, namely that an Assyrian soldier is shown ripping open a pregnant Arab woman in her tent. The scene would begin in the upper register (right tent) where a soldier would be slitting the woman's womb, and continue in the middle one (right tent) where he is removing the foetus from her belly. The lower register depicts the tent set on fire with the corpse of the woman lying on the floor. There is no written evidence which could directly confirm this interpretation, but note that the act of slitting the womb of pregnant women is mentioned in the royal hymn VAT 13833 (LKA 62) and in the Hebrew Bible (2Ki 8: 11–12, Am 1: 13 and Hos 14:1), see Cogan 1983.

[35] Not so easy as a human head weighs around five kilograms.

[36] For this subject see Russell 1991: 223–240.

FIGURE 6.11: SARGON GOUGING OUT THE EYES OF A PRISONER
(CAT.-NR. 13). FROM BOTTA AND FLANDIN 1849B: PL. 118.

FIGURE 6.10: ZINCIRLI STELE. ESARHADDON HOLDS TWO ROPES
ATTACHED TO RINGS PIERCED IN UŠ-ANAḪURU'S AND ABDI-MILKŪTI'S
LOWER LIPS (CAT.-NO 35). FROM BÖRKER-KLAHN 1982: NR. 218.

images can be understood, at least up to a certain point, by illiterates. While the theoretical audience in the case of iconographic sources includes all people who could see, the potential audience consists of a more reduced circle, depending on the accessibility of the pictures. We can distinguish between the following three groups (*Figure 6.14*):

1. The king and the royal family associated principally with the royal apartments in the more private wing of the palace (*bītānu*),
2. The Assyrian and foreign visitors related principally with the throne-room suite and the adjoining courtyard in the more official or public wing (*bābānu*), and
3. The servants, courtiers, and dignitaries who had more or less access to both wings.

When the king commissioned his artists to make wall reliefs or bronze bands for huge gates, he did undoubtedly not ignore that the potential audience would be much greater than that of the buried or displayed inscriptions. We must not forget that these works of art had another important – if not the most important – function, namely a decorative one. They were conceived for the pleasure of the king and to stress his greatness, as only the king was able to order such magnificent works of art. This does not mean that the reliefs were intended to be seen either as a whole or in detail by every person entering the palace. Such a possibility was highly reduced as it was a function of the context of the pictures.[37] The capability to see a certain depiction, especially a brutality scene, depended on the following factors:

1. The function of the rooms (which we know only roughly) determines the degree of accessibility for a certain person or group of persons. A brutality scene located at the wall of an audience room was potentially seen by more numerous and more different persons than a scene on the wall of a bathroom in a royal apartment.
2. The scale of the depictions influences the capability to discover or see at all a specific scene. It is not the same to stand in front of a plate with one register in superhuman scale (like some of Sargon's reliefs), or a plate with two registers, one meter each and separated by an inscription (like some Ashurnasirpal's reliefs), or plates some two meters high covered with huge battle scenes with hundreds of figures (Sennacherib,

---

[37] Even with good conditions of accessibility to the rooms and visibility of the displayed scenes, it must have been almost impossible for a visitor to notice all details of the wall reliefs - because of the monumental dimensions of the palace. Like modern tourists visiting the palace of Versailles, visitors would have been impressed by the greatness of the Assyrian palaces as a whole and noticed some details only by chance.

#[a]	No[b]	Atrocity	Anp	Slm	Tigl	Sg	Sn	Ash	Asb
Group A: Soldiers									
1	1	Corpses river				17–23[c]			45, 48–50, 52–53, 56
2	3	Heads city		5, 6, 7					
3	23	Heads inventory	1		9, 10, 12	16	24–28, 31–32		36–39, 41
Group B: Member of the elite									
4	10	Impalement		3, 4, 6	8	15	30		
5	11	Flaying				14	29		46
6	13	Grinding bones							40
7	14	Ring'n rope				13		33–35	
8	15	Tongue pulling							47
9	16	Beheading	2		11	17–23			42–44, 51, 55
10	18	Dismembering		6					
11	24	To gouge out the eyes				13			
Group C: Civilian population									
12	25	Rape (?)							54

[a] In this columns are the atrocities serially numbered; [b] The numbers in this column correspond to the types of atrocities (1 to 22) described for the royal inscriptions with three additional cases which are only attested in the iconographic material (23 to 25). [c] The numbers in the columns for each king refer to the catalogue (see Appendix).

FIGURE 6.12: BRUTALITY SCENES IN NEO-ASSYRIAN ART

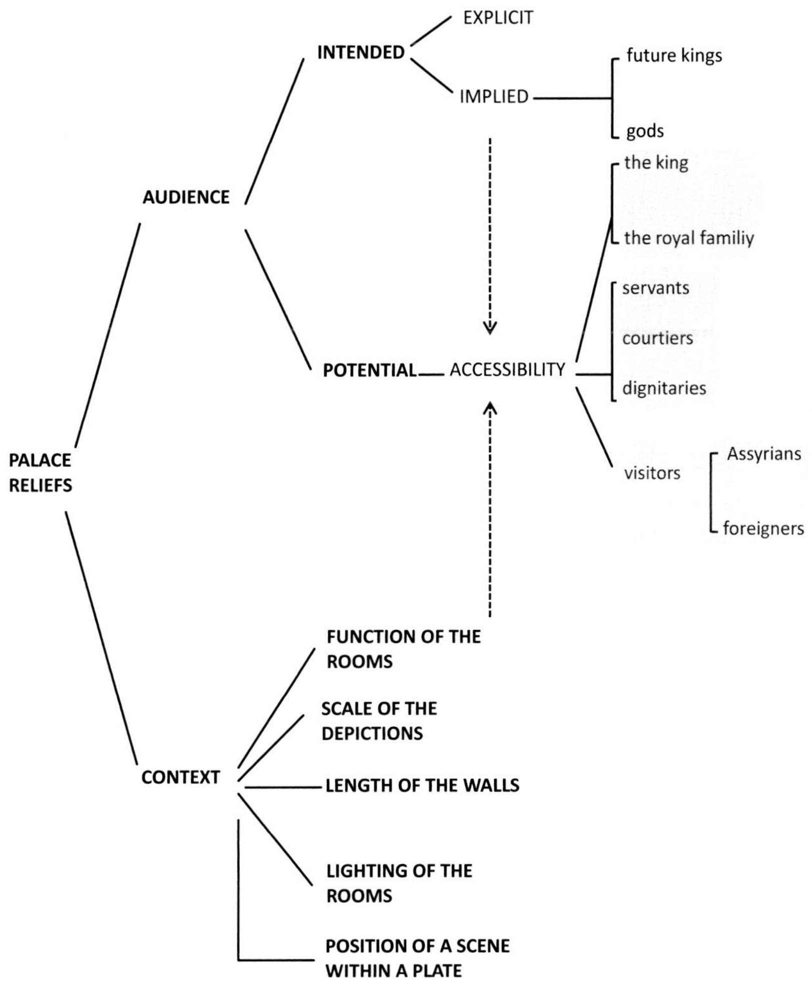

FIGURE 6.13: THE ADDRESSEES OF THE ICONOGRAPHIC SOURCES

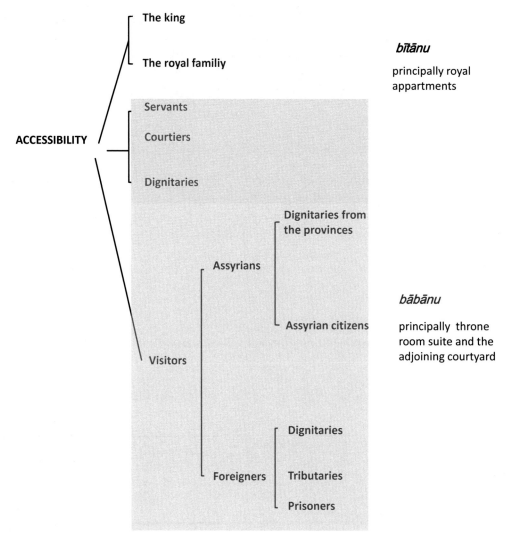

FIGURE 6.14: DEGREES OF ACCESSIBILITY TO THE PALACE RELIEFS

Ashurbanipal), or bronze bands with two 7 to 8.7 cm high registers.[38]

3. The length of the walls, namely the dimensions of a room, has a decisive impact on the perception of a specific detail like a brutality scene. Reliefs on a 5 meters long wall are undoubtedly more manageable than those on a more than forty meters long wall.

4. The lighting of the room is another essential factor, about which we unfortunately know very little. Open courtyards were longer and better illuminated than the rest of the rooms. We do not know how well and for how long the rooms of a palace were lighted, but it is realistic to assume that the conditions were not those of a modern museum. The lighting was probably not uniform among and inside the rooms, poor, and restricted to certain hours of the day. If a brutality scene was located in a part of a wall that was insufficiently illuminated, it would be probably very difficult or even impossible to discover it.

5. The position of a scene within the slab conditions its effectiveness and the possibility to see it at all. One thing is a brutality scene filling completely a square slab with a side-length of 3 metres, and another thing is a detail in the middle of a huge composition with multiple figures. Even if it was argued that such details were conceived as a kind of magnets to call the attention and force awareness,[39] first you must be able to discover them, and this was certainly not always the case. Now it is time to take a closer look at the brutality scenes in their context.

The brutality scenes in their context

A first interesting result (*Figure 6.15*) consists in the fact that brutality scenes were to be found not only in public places (Cat.-Nos 3–7, No 33–35) or in the more

---

[38] Unger 1913: 12. The total height of each band including the two registers and three rows of rosettes (each one 2–3cm high) ranges from 24.8 to 27.1cm, Curtis and Tallis 2008: 14, table 2.

[39] Reed 2007: 103 and 107–112.

King	More public wing/area	Throne room suite	More private wing	Context unknown
Anp	2	1[a] (throne room)		
Slm	3–7			
Tigl			11–12	8–10
Sg	13–23			
Sn	25(courtyard)	24 (hall)	26–27, 31, 28–30 (ceremonial?)	32
Esh	33–35			
Asb		54 (hall)	36–37 (courtyard), 38–49 (ceremonial?), 50–53	55–56
Total	21	3	26 (12 ceremonial)	6

[a] The numbers refer to the catalogue (see Appendix).

FIGURE 6. 15: LOCATION OF THE BRUTALITY SCENES

public wing of a palace (Cat.-Nos 1, 13–22, 24–25, 54), but also (26 cases against 24) in the more private wing (Cat.-Nos 11–12, 26–27, 31, 28–30, 36–49, 50–53). Even if in the private wing some rooms seem to have been used for ceremonial purposes, like in the case of the reception suite where the "Lachish Room" was located (Cat.-Nos 28–30, 38–49, altogether 15 cases), the access to this part of the palace was probably more restricted than that to the public wing. One third of the brutality scenes in the private wing (9 out of 26) were located in private apartments, which were occupied by the king, his family and probably some high dignitaries (Cat.-Nos 11–12, 26–27, 31, 50–53). One scene is even located in a bathroom (Cat.-No 50).

Leaving aside the scenes exposed outside a palace, namely on the palace gates of Balawat (Cat.-Nos 2–7) and on Esarhaddon's stelae from Til-Barsip and Zincirli (Cat.-Nos 33–35), only in fifteen cases were brutality scenes located in the public wing of a palace: three in the throne room suite (Cat.-Nos 1, 24, 54), one in an adjoining courtyard (Cat.-No 25) and eleven in a complex behind the royal apartments that was probably used for audiences in Sargon's palace (Cat.-Nos 13–23). The fact that the brutality scenes in the more private wing are almost twice as many as those in the more public wing (26 to 15) is a rough but clear indicator that not all the depictions of cruelties were intended to be seen by a wide public.

Besides the location and function of the rooms where they were placed, further factors restrict additionally the possibility to appreciate the brutality scenes, which were in most cases only details of a greater composition: the scale of the depictions, the length of the walls, and the position of a scene within the plate. Because of the possible combinations of those three factors there is a wide range of visibility conditions, but in most cases the impact is a negative one (*Figure 6.16*). As the reliefs could have from one to six registers, the greater the number of registers, the smaller was the scale (for instance the battle of the River Ulai in six registers, each some 40 cm

high, Cat.-Nos 44–45, *Figure 6.3*). Furthermore, a detail in the lower register was very difficult to see, as it was at lower leg height (for instance Nos 36–37, *Figure 6.5*). That foreign dignitaries kneeled or crouched down to find details seems improbable. Even brutality scenes on relief plates shaped in one register were not necessarily easy to find, as the whole surface might be covered by a hundred figures, as in the case of the relief showing the conquest of Lachish (Cat.-Nos 29–30, *Figures 6.7-8*). Furthermore the location of a detail in a corner (Cat.-No 24) or on a long wall (Cat.-Nos 1, 25, 26, 38, 39, 54; 20m to 47m) made it difficult to perceive the brutality scenes. In some cases they were probably only discovered by chance.

The exhibition of brutality scenes on an object outside a palace was no warrant for proper visibility. The most striking examples are the brutality scenes on the bronze bands which decorated Shalmaneser's palace gates in Imgur-Enlil/Balawat (*Figure 6.4*):[40] Most of these scenes depicting impalements, severed heads and mutilations, which are frequently quoted as a paradigmatic example for the alleged intimidation function of such scenes, were not only realized on a very small scale, but out of the visual field: with the exception of the second band, the remaining six upper rows were placed too high and could not be seen at all. We do not know with certainty the original distribution of the bands, but it is more than probable that most of those depicting cruelties were not reachable. On the other hand, in order to regard a detail from the lowest band, the observer should have been in face-down position, not the most elegant way to be before the palace.[41]

---

[40] Three sets of bronze bands were found in the citadel Balawat: one set belongs to the gates of the Mamu-Temple built by Ashurnasirpal II; the other two sets – dating to the time of Ashurnasirpal II and Shalmaneser III respectively – decorated two gates of a monumental building, probably a palace according to Oates 1974: 177 with pl. xxvi; see also Schachner 2007: 9–16 and Curtis and Tallis 2008: 16.

[41] In *Figure 6.4* I follow the arrangement of the bands as displayed in the British Museum and described by J. E. Curtis in Curtis and Tallis 2008: 14, table 2.1. Curtis rejects categorically the alternative reconstructions proposed by Hertel 2004 and Schachner 2007: 23–30

King	Clearly visible*	Visible	Very difficult	Impossible	Unknown
Anp		1ᵃ (long wall) T		2 PG	
Slm			5 OP	3–4, 6–7 PG	
Tigl		11–12 (long wall) Pr			8–10 Unk
Sg	13–14 Pu	16–22 (long wall), 23 (entrance)	15 (to low) Pu		
Sn		24 (corner) T, 25 (long wall) Pu 26 (long wall) Pr 27–28 Pr 31 Pr, 32 Unk	29–30 (small scale) Pr		
Esh	33 PC, 34–35 CG				
Asb		36–37 (low) Pr, 38–39 Pe/C, 50 Pr, 54 (long wall, low) T	40–49 (small scale) Pr/C, 51–53 (small scale) Pr/C,		55–56 Unk
Total	5	24	17	5	5

ᵃ The numbers refer to the catalogue (see Appendix).

Key

CG = City gate; PC = palace courtyard?; PG = Palace gates; Pr = More private wing of a palace; Pr/C = More private wing of a palace / Ceremonial function?; Pu = More public wing of a palace ; T = Throne room suite; Unk = Function of the room or room unknown; * = clearly intimidation message.

FIGURE 6.16: VISIBILITY OF THE BRUTALITY SCENES

Nevertheless, there are indeed some few cases where a brutality scene was depicted on a sufficient scale and in an accessible place or position that let no doubts about the intimidating character of the message. The most striking example and the only one in the homeland are two huge plates (3m high by 4m wide) in one of the rooms of the so called *Festflügel* of Sargon's palace in Dūr-Šarrukēn (Cat.-Nos 13–14). Room 8 is one of two large rooms (35m long by 8m wide) which may have been used for audiences. It has the particularity that a pedestal was located at the smaller side opposite the entrance, probably where the throne stood. On the wall, directly behind the pedestal, a huge relief depicts the king gouging a prisoner, who stands on his knees and is held with a rope attached to a ring pierced in his mouth (*Figure 6.11*). The intention of the depiction is in this case more than clear, and another image on one of the longer walls reinforces it: two soldiers are shown flaying a prisoner. Whether the palace was ever inhabited and the images were viewed by anyone remains an open question.

Esarhaddon's Til-Barsip (Cat.-No 34) and Zincirli (Cat.-No 35, *Figure 6.10*) stelae, found in or near a city gate, and a second stela from Til-Barsip found inside the Assyrian palace and perhaps erected in a courtyard (Cat.-No 33) also show in great format the king holding two defeated rulers (the Egyptian crown prince Uš-Anaḫuru and the Sidonian king Abdi-Milqūti) with a rope attached to rings pierced in their lower lips. The usual character of this kind of monument as a reminder to foreign rulers what

may happen if they rebel against the Assyrian king was in these cases explicitly displayed. The last example are two depictions in the wall paintings from the Assyrian palace in Til-Barsip dating probably to the time of Tiglath-pileser: one shows the execution by a cut in a prisoner's throat in the presence of other Arabian prisoners (Cat.-No 11 from room XXIV),[42] and a second one, only fragmentarily preserved, depicts a giant Assyrian warrior surrounded by severed heads (Cat.-No 12 from room XLVII). The scenes were 1.50m and 1.30m high respectively and well visible at eye-level as they were elevated from the floor by a 50cm high frieze. However each room was part of an apartment in the more private wing of the palace, and it is possible that one of them (where room XXIV was located) was the royal apartment – a feature that would extremely reduce the number of potential visitors.

The cruelties shown on Sargon's reliefs and Esarhaddon's stelae were clearly intended to warn foreigners about the consequences of insurrection against the Assyrian authority, but they represent exceptions which confirm the rule: the brutality scenes were mostly details, not always easy to be seen or accessed, and were, like the descriptions in the royal inscriptions, not primarily intended to intimidate but were only part of magnificent reliefs that could only be commissioned by a powerful king, against whom one should be extremely careful not to rebel.

[42] Beheading was the second step. It was not possible to behead a prisoner with the swords available at that time nor in the depicted position. After the cut in the throat the victim fainted, and once he lay on the ground the executor could begin the hard task of cutting his head. For beheading in the Ancient Near East see Dolce 2014.

(especially 28, table 6), Curtis and Tallis 2008: 13–15.

Conclusions

The catalogue of brutal acts committed by Assyrian soldiers after a battle or siege is long and impressive. As the Assyrians were more powerful and successful than their adversaries they had more opportunities to punish them, but brutality was not an exclusively Assyrian feature, neither in the context of the Ancient Near East nor in that of the history of mankind. They were of course brutal but not more so than others, and therefore we should rather speak of brutalities committed by the Assyrians than of Assyrian brutality. Brutal punishments after the submission of the enemy were neither implemented after every victory in every campaign nor were they an aleatory act. They were a structural component of the Assyrian domination policy and were applied with an intimidating character to dissuade foreign rulers from rebellion against the Assyrian dominion. The brutal acts were directed against soldiers and members of the elite and seldom against the civilian population. The narrative accounts in the royal inscriptions mention brutalities and the narrative reliefs show them as part of the military campaigns described in the texts and depicted on the palace walls. The acts themselves had an intimidation function, but not their descriptions and depictions. As most of the royal inscriptions were buried and the displayed ones could hardly be read by a mainly illiterate audience, the existence of propaganda is out of the question, as there was no public for it. This applies also to a great part of the brutality scenes, which were only apparently more accessible for an audience. The degree of accessibility to the palace rooms, the scale and position of the images as well as the dimensions and lighting conditions of the rooms affected dramatically the degree of visibility of those scenes, which were in most cases only details within a huge composition. In a few cases the brutality scenes were in fact intended as a warning, but those are the exceptions which confirm the rule.[43]

---

[43] The fact that the description and depiction of brutalities were not primarily intended to intimidate the enemy does not change the atrocious character of Assyrian warfare. Furthermore, as argued above, cruelty was not exclusively an Assyrian feature. However it must be noted that the fact that they mentioned – in some cases in detail – brutality acts in their inscriptions and depicted them on reliefs, namely that they recognized brutality as part of the imperial policy and did not hesitate to write about it or show it, may be considered a particular feature of the Assyrian kings and elite members. So many and so thoroughly described atrocities cannot be found in any other corpus of Ancient Near Eastern royal inscriptions, for instance the Neo-Babylonian ones. On the other hand, the absence of detailed descriptions of brutalities cannot simply be interpreted as an indication of less brutal warfare and handling of the enemy. It suffices to remember that, after the conquest of Jerusalem in 586, Nebuchadnezzar II let slay the sons of the Judaean king Zedekiah before their father, then put out his eyes and led him in chains to Babylon (2Ki 25: 8).

References

Barnett, R. D. 1976. *Sculptures from the North Palace of Ashurbanipal at Nineveh*. Oxford.

Barnett, R. D., Bleibtreu, E. and Turner, G. 1998. *Sculptures from the Southwest Palace of Sennacherib at Nineveh*. London.

Barnett, R. D. and Falkner, M. 1962. *The Sculptures of Assur-Nasir-Apli II (883–859 B.C.), Tiglath-Pileser III (745–727 B.C.) and Esarhaddon (681–669 B.C.) from the Central and South-West Palaces at Nimrud*. London.

Bauer, Th. 1933. *Das Inschriftenwerk Assurbanipals*. Leipzig.

Bleibtreu, E. 1991. Grisly Assyrian Record of Torture and Death. *BAR* 17/1: 52–61, 75.

J. Börker-Klähn, *Altvorderasiatische Bildstelen und vergleichbare Felsreliefs*, BaF 4. Mainz am Rhein.

Botta, P. E. and Flandin, E. 1849. *Monument de Ninive I*. London.

Botta/Flandin 1849b. *Monument de Ninive II*. London.

Cogan, M. 1983. "Ripping Open Pregnant Women" in Light of an Assyrian Analogue. *JAOS* 103:755–757.

Curtis, J. E. and Tallis, N. 2008. *The Balawat Gates of Ashurnasirpal II*. London.

Dolce, R. 2004. The "Head of the enemy" in the Sculptures from the Palaces of Nineveh: An Example of "Cultural Migration"?. *Iraq* 66: 121–132.

Dolce, R. 2014. *Perdere la testa". Aspetti e valori della decapitazione nel Vicino Oriente Antico*. Rome.

Dubowsky, P. 2009. Ripping Pen Pregnant Arab Women: Reliefs in Room L of Ashurbanipal's North Palace. *Or NS* 78: 394–419.

Fuchs, A. 2009. Waren die Assyrer grausam? In M. Zimmermann (ed), *Extreme Formen der Gewalt in Bild und Text des Altertums*: 65–119. München.

Gadd, C. J. 1936. *The Stones of Assyria*. London.

Hertel, T. 2004. The Balawat Gate narratives of Shalmaneser III. In J. G. Dercksen (ed), *Assyria and Beyond. Studies Presented to Mogens Trolle Larsen*: 209–315. Leiden.

Jacobs, B. 2009. Grausame Hinrichtungen – friedliche Bilder. Zum Verhältnis der politischen Realität zu den Darstellungsszenarien der achämenidischen Kunst. In M. Zimmermann (ed), *Extreme Formen der Gewalt in Bild und Text des Altertums*: 121–154. München.

Landsberger, B. 1989. The political testament of Sennacherib. In H. Tadmor, B. Landsberger and S. Parpola (eds), *The Sin of Sargon and Sennacherib's Last Will*, SAAB 3: 3–51 (written in 1967). Helsinki.

Layard, A. H. 1853. *The Monuments of Nineveh I*. London.

Meuszyński, J. 1981. *Die Rekonstruktion der Reliefdarstellungen und ihrer Anordnung im Nordwestpalast von Kalḫu (Nimrūd)*, BaF 2. Mainz am Rhein.

Oates, D. 1974. Balawat (Imgur-Enlil): The Site and Its Buildings. *Iraq* 36: 173-178.

Oppenheim, A. L. 1960. The City of Aššur in 714 BC. *JNES* 19: 133-147.

Orthmann, W. 1985. *Propyläen Kunstgeschichte*, Der Alte Orient 14. Berlin.

Villard, P. 1988. Les structures du récit et les relations entre texte et image dans les bas-reliefs néo-assyriens. *Word & Image. A Journal of Verbal/Visual Enquiry* 4/1: 422–429.

Weippert, M. 1973-74. Die Kämpfe des assyrischen Königs Assurbanipal gegen die Araber, *WO* 7: 39–85.

Appendix: Catalogue of brutality scenes in Neo-Assyrian art[44]

No 1

Date:	Anp II
Type:	Wall relief
Dimensions:	88 x 208
Signature:	BM 124550
Publication:	Layard 1853: pl. 22 (drawing); Gadd 1936: 135–136 (photo).
Provenance:	Nimrud (Kalhu)
Location:	Northwest Palace, room B, upper register; see Meuszyński 1981: pl. 2, B-6.
Description:	Soldiers carrying and playing with heads.

No 2

Date:	Anp II
Type:	Bronze band relief
Dimensions:	18.3 (total height with two friezes of rosettes)
Signature:	BM 124686
Publication:	Curtis and Tallis 2008: 111, fig.10 (drawing) and 110, fig. 9 (photo)
Provenance:	Balawat (Imgur-Enlil)
Location:	Palace (?) gate, band L2 (second band from the top)
Description:	The beheaded body of an enemy lies under an Assyrian chariot.

No 3

Date:	Slm III
Type:	Bronze band relief
Dimensions:	7 to 8.7cm (register height without the rows of rosettes); band height 26.45
Signature:	BM 124659
Publication:	Schachner 2007: 294, pl. 2 (drawing) and 313, fig. 21a (photo).
Provenance:	Balawat (Imgur-Enlil)
Location:	Palace (?) gate, Band II (R5), upper register, 51–50
Description:	Impalement

No 4

Date:	Slm III
Type:	Bronze band relief
Dimensions:	7 to 8.7cm (register height without the rows of rosettes); band height 27.00
Signature:	BM 124661
Publication:	Schachner 2007: 296, pl. 4 (drawing) and 321, fig. 29a (photo)
Provenance:	Balawat (Imgur-Enlil)
Location:	Palace (?) gate, Band IV (R3), lower register, 43–47
Description:	Impalement

No 5

Date:	Slm III
Type:	Bronze band relief
Dimensions:	7 to 8.7cm (register height without the rows of rosettes); band height 26.80
Publication:	Schachner 2007: 300, pl. 8 (drawing) and 334, fig. 42a (photo)

---

[44] Dimensions (height x width) in cm. Dating of the reliefs in the Southwest Palace according to Russell 1991:151.

Signature: BM 124657
Provenance: Balawat (Imgur-Enlil)
Location: Palace (?) gate, Band VIII (R8), lower register, 24
Description: Piles of heads in front of a city.

No 6
Date: Slm III
Type: Bronze band relief
Dimensions: 7 to 8.7cm (register height without the rows of rosettes); band height 26.80
Signature: BM 124653
Publication: Schachner 2007: pl. 10 (drawing) and 340–341, figs. 48b–49a (photo)
Provenance: Balawat (Imgur-Enlil)
Location: Palace (?) gate, Band X (L4), lower register, 16–19 and 20
Description: Mutilation and impalement of prisoners; severed heads around the city wall.

No 7
Date: Slm III
Type: Bronze band relief
Dimensions: 7 to 8.7cm (register height without the rows of rosettes); band height 27.10
Signature: BM 124660
Publication: Schachner 2007: 305, pl. 13 (drawing) and 352, fig. 60a (photo)
Provenance: Balawat (Imgur-Enlil)
Location: Palace (?) gate, Band XIII (R6), upper register, 55
Description: Heads along a city wall.

No 8
Date: Tigl III
Type: Wall relief
Dimensions: 109 x 109
Signature: BM 118903
Publication: Barnett and Falkner 1962: pl. xxxix (photo)
Provenance: Nimrud (Kalḫu)
Location: Central Palace, series B, upper register, slab 15a, relief 19
Description: Impalement

No 9
Date: Tigl III
Type: Wall relief
Dimensions: 102.5 x 75.0
Signature: Zürich 1919
Publication: Barnett and Falkner 1962: pl. xlvii (drawing) and xlix (photo)
Provenance: Nimrud (Kalḫu)
Location: Central Palace, series B, upper register, slab 17b, relief 22
Description: Soldiers bringing heads to a dignitary.

No 10
Date: Tigl III
Type: Wall relief
Dimensions: –
Signature: Or.Dr. I, 9
Publication: Barnett and Falkner 1962: pl. lix (drawing)
Provenance: Nimrud (Kalḫu)
Location: Between the Central Palace and the upper chambers
Description: Soldier bringing heads and a prisoner before the king.

No 11
Date: Tigl III
Type: Wall painting

Dimensions: 150.7 x 328.7
Signature: –
Publication: Thureau-Dangin and Dunand 1936: pl. li (monochrome); Parrot 1961: 107, fig. 116 (colour) and 106, fig. 115 (detail)
Provenance: Tell Asmar (Til Barsip)
Location: Assyrian palace, room xxiv, some 50cm above the floor (*plinthe asphaltée*)
Description: Execution of a prisoner.

No 12
Date: Tigl III
Type: Wall painting
Dimensions: 130.10 x 191.8
Signature: –
Publication: Thureau-Dangin and Dunand 1936: pl. lii (monochrome); Parrot 1961: fig. 1 before page 1 (detail, colour)
Provenance: Tell Asmar (Til Barsip)
Location: Assyrian palace, room xlvii, some 50cm above the floor (*plinthe asphaltée*)
Description: Assyrian warrior surrounded by severed heads; another severed head lies between the legs of second warrior.

No 13
Date: Sg
Type: Wall relief
Dimensions: approx. 300.0 x 430.0
Signature: –
Publication: Botta and Flandin 1849b: pl. 118 (drawing)
Provenance: Khorsabad (Dūr-Šarrukēn)
Location: Palace, room 8, slab 12
Description: The king gouging out the eyes of a prisoner held by a rope attached to a ring pierced in his lower lip.

No 14
Date: Sg
Type: Wall relief
Dimensions: approx. 300.0 x 430.0
Signature: –
Publication: Botta and Flandin 1849b: pl. 120 (drawing)
Provenance: Khorsabad (Dūr-Šarrukēn)
Location: Palace, room 8, slabs 24–25
Description: Flaying of a prisoner.

No 15
Date: Sg
Type: Wall relief
Dimensions: approx. 120 x 250 (lower register), approx. total height 290 (two registers with inscription between them)
Signature: –
Publication: Botta and Flandin 1849a: pl. 55 (drawing)
Provenance: Khorsabad (Dūr-Šarrukēn)
Location: Palace, room 2, slab 7, lower register
Description: Impalement of 14 prisoners.

No 16
Date: Sg
Type: Wall relief
Dimensions: approx. 120 x 250 (lower register), approx. total height 290 (two registers with inscription between them)
Signature: –
Publication: Botta and Flandin 1849a: pl. 54 (drawing)

Provenance:	Khorsabad (Dūr-Šarrukēn)
Location:	Palace, room 2, slab 3, lower register
Description:	Pile of severed heads before dignitaries? (poorly preserved).

No 17

Date:	Sg
Type:	Wall relief
Dimensions:	approx. 120 x 250 (lower register), approx. total height 290 (two registers with inscription between them)
Signature:	–
Publication:	Botta and Flandin 1849a: pl. 61 (drawing)
Provenance:	Khorsabad (Dūr-Šarrukēn)
Location:	Palace, room 2, slab 14, lower register
Description:	Beheaded bodies before a conquered city.

No 18

Date:	Sg
Type:	Wall relief
Dimensions:	approx. 120 x 250 (lower register), approx. total height 290 (two registers with inscription between them)
Signature:	–
Publication:	Botta and Flandin 1849a: pl. 63 (drawing)
Provenance:	Khorsabad (Dūr-Šarrukēn)
Location:	Palace, room 2, slab 16, lower register
Description:	Beheaded bodies in the battle field.

No 19

Date:	Sg
Type:	Wall relief
Dimensions:	approx. 120 x 250 (lower register), approx. total height 290 (two registers with inscription between them)
Signature:	–
Publication:	Botta and Flandin 1849a: pl. 64 (drawing)
Provenance:	Khorsabad (Dūr-Šarrukēn)
Location:	Palace, room 2, slab 17, lower register
Description:	Beheaded bodies before a conquered city.

No 20

Date:	Sg
Type:	Wall relief
Dimensions:	approx. 120 x 250 (lower register), approx. total height 290 (two registers with inscription between them)
Signature:	–
Publication:	Botta and Flandin 1849a: pl. 65 (drawing)
Provenance:	Khorsabad (Dūr-Šarrukēn)
Location:	Palace, room 2, slab 18, lower register
Description:	Beheaded bodies in the battle field.

No 21

Date:	Sg
Type:	Wall relief
Dimensions:	approx. 120 x 250 (lower register), approx. total height 290 (two registers with inscription between them)
Signature:	–
Publication:	Botta and Flandin 1849a: pl. 66 (drawing)
Provenance:	Khorsabad (Dūr-Šarrukēn)
Location:	Palace, room 2, slab 19, lower register
Description:	Beheaded bodies in the battle field.

No 22

Date:	Sg
Type:	Wall relief
Dimensions:	approx. 120 x 250 (lower register), approx. total height 290 (two registers with inscription between them)
Signature:	–
Publication:	Botta and Flandin 1849a: pl. 67 (drawing)
Provenance:	Khorsabad (Dūr-Šarrukēn)
Location:	Palace, room 2, slabs 20–21, lower register
Description:	Beheaded bodies in the battle field.

No 23

Date:	Sg
Type:	Wall relief
Dimensions:	approx. 120 x 250 (lower register), approx. total height 290 (two registers with inscription between them)
Signature:	–
Publication:	Botta and Flandin 1849a: pl. 76 (drawing)
Provenance:	Khorsabad (Dūr-Šarrukēn)
Location:	Palace, room 2 gate H, slab I, lower register
Description:	Beheaded bodies before a conquered city.

No 24

Date:	Sn
Type:	Wall relief
Dimensions:	–
Signature:	Or.Dr. IV, 14
Publication:	Barnett, Bleibtreu and Turner 1998: pl. 56 (drawing)
Provenance:	Nineveh
Location:	Southwest Palace, room V, 51a (slab 7 right), second register from the top
Description:	Soldiers bringing severed heads for inventory

No 25

Date:	Sn
Type:	Wall relief
Dimensions:	–
Signature:	Or.Dr. I, 70
Publication:	Barnett, Bleibtreu and Turner 1998: pl. 83 (drawing)
Provenance:	Nineveh
Location:	Southwest Palace, court VI, 102a (slab 11)
Description:	Soldiers bringing severed heads for inventory.

No 26

Date:	Sn
Type:	Wall relief
Dimensions:	approx. 382 x 650 (according to the scale of the drawing)
Signature:	Or.Dr. I, 63
Publication:	Barnett, Bleibtreu and Turner 1998: pl. 131–132 (drawing)
Provenance:	Nineveh
Location:	Southwest Palace, room VII, 193a (slabs 13–14), lower register
Description:	Soldiers bringing severed heads for inventory.

No 27

Date:	Sn
Type:	Wall relief
Dimensions:	173.3 x 165.7
Signature:	BM 124786b
Publication:	Barnett, Bleibtreu and Turner 1998: pl. 176 (drawing) and pl. 175 (photo)

Provenance:	Nineveh
Location:	Southwest Palace, room XIV, 244a (slab 14)
Description:	Soldiers carrying severed heads.

No 28

Date:	Sn
Type:	Wall relief
Dimensions:	172.7 x 175.2
Signature:	124903
Publication:	Barnett, Bleibtreu and Turner 1998: pl. 278 (drawing) and pl. 279 (photo)
Provenance:	Nineveh
Location:	Southwest Palace, room XXXII, 370a (slab 8)
Description:	Soldiers carrying severed heads.

No 29

Date:	Sn
Type:	Wall relief
Dimensions:	269.0 x 180.3 (slab 9), 254.8 x 101.6 (slab 10)
Signature:	BM 120908, BM 120909
Signature:	Barnett, Bleibtreu and Turner 1998: pl. 338 (drawing) and pl. 339 (photo)
Provenance:	Nineveh
Location:	Southwest Palace, room XXXVI, 432a (slab 9 right) and 433a (slab10 corner)
Description:	Flaying of two prisoners.

No 30

Date:	Sn
Type:	Wall relief
Dimensions:	167.6 x 190.5
Signature:	BM 124906
Publication:	Barnett, Bleibtreu and Turner 1998: pl. 330 (drawing) and pl. 331 (photo)
Provenance:	Nineveh
Location:	Southwest Palace, room XXXVI, 430a (slab 7)
Description:	Siege of Lachish. Impalement of three prisoners.

No 31

Date:	Sn
Type:	Wall relief
Dimensions:	–
Signature:	Or.Dr. IV, 24
Publication:	Barnett, Bleibtreu and Turner 1998: pl. 380 (drawing)
Provenance:	Nineveh
Location:	Southwest Palace, room XLV, 487a (slab 4)
Description:	Soldiers carrying severed heads.

No 32

Date:	Sn
Type:	Wall relief
Dimensions:	72 x 111.8 (fragment)
Signature:	Or.Dr. I, 49; Ashmolean Museum 1933.1575 (fragment)
Publication:	Barnett, Bleibtreu and Turner 1998: pl. 464 (drawing) and pl. 465 (photo)
Provenance:	Nineveh
Location:	Southwest Palace, room LXX, 645a (s3)
Description:	Soldiers carrying severed heads for inventory.

No 33

Date:	Esh
Type:	Stele
Dimensions:	380 x 172 x 60

Signatur:	Aleppo Museum 31
Publication:	Börker-Klahn 1982: Nr. 217 (drawing) and Parrot 1961: 77, fig. 86 (photo)
Provenance:	Tell Asmar (Til-Barsip)
Location:	Assyrian Palace
Description:	Esarhaddon holds two ropes attached to rings pierced in Uš-Anahuru's and Abdi-Milkūti's lower lips.

No 34

Date:	Esh
Type:	Stele
Dimensions:	330 x 166 x 66
Signatur:	Aleppo Museum 47
Publication:	Börker-Klahn 1982: Nr. 218 (drawing)
Provenance:	Tell Asmar (Til-Barsip)
Location:	Near the Lion's Gate
Description:	Esarhaddon holds two ropes attached to rings pierced in Uš-Anahuru's and Abdi-Milkūti's lower lips.

No 35

Date:	Esh
Type:	Stele
Dimensions:	318.0 x 135.0 x 62 (left side)
Signature:	VA 2708
Publication:	Börker-Klahn 1982: Nr. 219 (drawing) and Orthmann 1985: pl. 232 (photo)
Provenance:	Zincirli (Sam'alla)
Location:	Chamber of a city gate (*in situ*)
Description:	Esarhaddon holds two ropes attached to rings pierced in Uš-Anahuru's and Abdi-Milkūti's lower lips (same scene as No 24 and 25, side-inverted)

No 36

Date:	Asb
Type:	Wall relief
Dimensions:	99 x approx. 150 (fragment)
Signature:	BM 124782a
Publication:	Barnett, Bleibtreu and Turner 1998: pl. 193 (drawing) and pl. 195 (photo)
Provenance:	Nineveh
Location:	Southwest Palace, court XIX, 277a (slab 19)
Description:	Soldiers carrying severed heads for inventory.

No 37

Date:	Asb
Type:	Wall relief
Dimensions:	232.4 x 204.4
Signature:	BM 124825c
Publication:	Barnett, Bleibtreu and Turner 1998: pl. 210 (drawing) and pl. 211 (photo)
Provenance:	Nineveh
Location:	Southwest Palace, court XIX, 284a (slab 10)
Description:	Soldiers carrying severed heads for inventory.

No 38

Date:	Asb
Type:	Wall relief
Dimensions:	96.5 x 154.9
Signature:	Or.Dr. IV, 36; BM 124477e (fragment; very few from upper register is preserved)
Publication:	Barnett, Bleibtreu and Turner 1998: pl. 244 (drawing) and pl. 245 (photo)
Provenance:	Nineveh
Location:	Southwest Palace, room XXVIII, 342a (slabs 6 and 6a)
Description:	Soldiers carrying severed heads for inventory.

No 39

Date:	Asb
Type:	Wall relief
Dimensions:	152.4 x 163.2 (slab 9); 134.6 x 109.2 (slab 10)
Signature:	BM 124955; BM 124956
Publication:	Barnett, Bleibtreu and Turner 1998: pl. 252 (drawing) and pl. 253 (photo)
Provenance:	Nineveh
Location:	Southwest Palace, room XXVIII, 346a (slabs 9 and 10), lower register (slab 9)
Description:	Soldiers carrying severed heads for inventory.

No 40

Date:	Asb
Type:	Wall relief
Dimensions:	180.3 x 200.6
Signature:	BM 124801a
Publication:	Barnett, Bleibtreu and Turner 1998: pl. 288 (drawing) and pl. 289 (photo)
Provenance:	Nineveh
Location:	Southwest Palace, room XXXIII, 381 (slab 1), upper register
Description:	The sons of Nabû-šuma-ēreš, the governor of Nippur, grinding his father's bones.

No 41

Date:	Asb
Dimensions:	180.3 x 200.6
Signature:	BM 124801a
Type:	Wall relief
Publication:	Barnett, Bleibtreu and Turner 1998: pl. 288 (drawing) and pl. 289 (photo)
Provenance:	Nineveh
Location:	Southwest Palace, room XXXIII, 381 (s1), second register from the top, right side
Description:	Soldiers carrying severed heads for inventory.

No 42

Date:	Asb
Type:	Wall relief
Dimensions:	180.3 x 200.6
Signature:	BM 124801a
Publication:	Barnett, Bleibtreu and Turner 1998: pl. 288 (drawing) and pl. 289 (photo)
Provenance:	Nineveh
Location:	Southwest Palace, room XXXIII, 381 (s1), second register from the top, left side
Description:	A soldier holds Teumman's severed head over a chariot.

No 43

Date:	Asb
Type:	Wall relief
Dimensions:	147.3 x 175.2
Signature:	BM 124801b
Publication:	Barnett, Bleibtreu and Turner 1998: pl. 292 (drawing) and pl. 293 (photo)
Provenance:	Nineveh
Location:	Southwest Palace, room XXXIII, 382a (slab 2), middle register
Description:	A soldier holds Teumman's severed head near another soldier who executes Itunî, the eunuch of the Elamite king.

No 44

Date:	Asb
Type:	Wall relief
Dimensions:	208.3 x 175.3
Signature:	BM 124801c
Publication:	Barnett, Bleibtreu and Turner 1998: pl. 296 (drawing) and pl. 297 (photo)
Provenance:	Nineveh

Location: Southwest Palace, room XXXIII, 383a (slab 3), second register from the bottom, left side
Description: A soldier holds Teumman's severed head.

No 45
Date: Asb
Type: Wall relief
Dimensions: 208.3 x 175.3
Signature: BM 124801c
Publication: Barnett, Bleibtreu and Turner 1998: pl. 296 (drawing) and pl. 297 (photo)
Provenance: Nineveh
Location: Southwest Palace, room XXXIII, 383a (slab 3), lower half of the slab, right side
Description: Defeated Elamite soldiers are thrown into the River Ulai.

No 46
Date: Asb
Type: Wall relief
Dimensions: 269.3 x 142.2
Signature: BM 124802a
Publication: Barnett, Bleibtreu and Turner 1998: pl. 300 (drawing) and pl. 301 (photo)
Provenance: Nineveh
Location: Southwest Palace, room XXXIII, 384a (slab 4)
Description: Soldiers flay prisoners while another one holds a severed head (second register from the top).

No 47
Date: Asb
Type: Wall relief
Dimensions: 269.3 x 142.2
Signature: BM 124802a
Publication: Barnett, Bleibtreu and Turner 1998: pl. 300 (drawing) and pl. 301 (photo)
Provenance: Nineveh
Location: Southwest Palace, room XXXIII, 384a (slab 4)
Description: Soldiers pull out the tongue of prisoners (third register from the top).

No 48
Date: Asb
Type: Wall relief
Dimensions: 264.4 x 154.9
Signature: BM 124802b
Publication: Barnett, Bleibtreu and Turner 1998: pl. 304 (drawing) and pl. 305 (photo)
Provenance: Nineveh
Location: Southwest Palace, room XXXIII, 385a (slab 5), lowest register
Description: Mutilated corpses floating in a river.

No 49
Date: Asb
Type: Wall relief
Dimensions: 269.2 x 152.4
Signature: BM 124802c
Publication: Barnett, Bleibtreu and Turner 1998: pl. 308 (drawing) and pl. 309 (photo)
Provenance: Nineveh
Location: Southwest Palace, room XXXIII, 386a (slab 6), lowest register
Description: Mutilated corpses floating in a river.

No 50
Date: Asb
Type: Wall relief
Dimensions: 228.6 x 215.9 (slab 3), 228.6 x 241.3 (slab 4)
Signature: BM 121931, BM 121932

Publication:	Barnett 1976: pl. xvii (photo)
Provenance:	Nineveh
Location:	North Palace, room F, north-east wall, slabs 3–4
Description:	Mutilated corpses floating in a river.

No 51

Date:	Asb
Type:	Wall relief
Dimensions:	68.6 x 83.8 (fragment)
Signature:	BM 124941
Publication:	Barnett 1976: pl. xxiv (photo)
Provenance:	Nineveh
Location:	North Palace, room I, slab 1 (part of lower register)
Description:	Beheaded corpses lay in the battlefield around the execution scene of Itunî, the eunuch of Teumman.

No 52

Date:	Asb
Type:	Wall relief
Dimensions:	–
Signature:	Or.Dr. VII, 11
Publication:	Barnett 1976: pl. xxv (drawing)
Provenance:	Nineveh
Location:	North Palace, room I, slab 6
Description:	Mutilated corpses floating in a river.

No 53

Date:	Asb
Type:	Wall relief
Dimensions:	–
Signature:	Or.Dr. VII, 11
Publication:	Barnett 1976: pl. xxv (drawing)
Provenance:	Nineveh
Location:	North Palace, room I, slab 7
Description:	Mutilated corpses floating in a river.

No 54

Date:	Asb
Type:	Wall relief
Dimensions:	137 x 162.6
Signature:	BM 124927
Publication:	Barnett 1976: pl. xxxiii (photo)
Provenance:	Nineveh
Location:	North Palace, room L, slab 9 (middle register)
Description:	Soldiers raping (?) a woman (middle register, right scene) or ripping open a pregnant woman (?).

No 55

Date:	Asb
Type:	Wall relief
Dimensions:	140 x 58.5 (BM 124920)
Signature:	Or.Dr. IV, 42 and 46; BM 124920 (slab c, upper register)
Publication:	Barnett 1976: pl. lxiii (drawing) and pl. lxiv (photo)
Provenance:	Nineveh
Location:	North Palace, room S¹ (fallen into room S), slabs b–c
Description:	Ashurbanipal and his queen banqueting in a garden showing Teumman's head hanging from a tree.

No 56

Date:	Asb
Type:	Wall relief

Dimensions:	44 x 52.5 (fragment)
Signature:	Vatican 14999
Publication:	Barnett 1976: pl. lxxii (photo)
Provenance:	Nineveh
Location:	North Palace, fragments gg and hh
Description:	Mutilated corpses floating in a river.

Images of War in the Assyrian Period:
What They Show and What They Hide

Davide Nadali[*]

Speaking of iconographies of war in the Ancient Near East immediately -it could be even said automatically- recalls to mind the huge amount of pictures of war of the Assyrian period. In fact, each Assyrian king recorded his military deeds and success in sculptures in the royal residences of the Assyrian capitals, mainly dealing with the visual narratives of his campaigns of conquest, fights and sieges.[1]

Taking into consideration the political efforts of the Assyrian kings in waging and managing war, the quantity of scenes of warfare is correctly balanced and reasonable: one can conclude that the depiction of the results of a military campaign, in general, or of a specific battle, more in detail, is the final accomplishment sealing the outcome of war. Beyond the specific and immediate antiquarian meaning and contribution to the study of the ancient Assyrian military system, I will try to linger on the political meaning of the systematic registration of military events in pictures trying to get a synthesis of the depiction of war and thus the importance of the iconography of war in the Assyrian world.

Summarising past studies on Assyrian warfare, attention has been principally given to specific and detailed aspects of the Assyrian military life using both textual and iconographic sources to describe the common weaponry, the dimension of the Assyrian army through the centuries and, most recently, the strategies and tactics of the Assyrian army to conquer cities in siege operations and confront the enemies in open field battles:[2] pictures of war on the Assyrian bas-reliefs have been used as a comprehensive catalogue of weapons, armour and war engines of the Assyrian soldiers, distinguishing categories of men, corps and units and analysing the change caused by the introduction of horse and the evolution of chariots in war context.[3]

All these past and recent aspects of the research on Assyrian warfare give us a technical and practical description of the way of waging war in the Assyrian period, with a faithful reconstruction of the size and management of the army, the effects of the weapons used against the enemies, and the outcome of the strategy employed by the Assyrians (according to nature of the terrain, strength of the enemy and possibility of success). Nevertheless, some aspects are still hidden and unknown since images principally focus on the culminating moment of the battle with the representation of the direct confrontation between the Assyrian army and its enemy. We must necessarily resort to the written evidence of the rich and large corpus of letters to detect and reveal those hidden aspects of the war, that is all activities and operation of preparation for a military campaign and the organisation of a battle starting from the enrolment of soldiers, their equipment, the construction of war machines and engines, the intervention of specialised corps of the Assyrian army (as, for example, the pioneers working in demolishing the fortification walls of the enemy city and working the battering rams).[4] Images of war make us see the war from outside; letters and other written evidence can make us see the war from within: as a significant example, when we look at the strong and heavy war machines climbing up the ramps built against the walls of the besieged cities, we can clearly recognize the single parts that have been assembled to build the war engine. But, how did it work inside? Which was the mechanism moving the tongue of the battering ram? And how were those machines moved?[5] Maybe groups of specialised soldiers, a well trained equip of men, manoeuvred the machine, but how they acted in the inner space and according to which system is obviously impossible to know. In this precise example, even written sources do not add specific details; as a consequence, hypotheses and reconstructions on the inner composition and functioning of battering rams can be forwarded as mere speculation based on comparisons with similar machines used in other periods, even distant in time from the Assyrians.

Images of warfare can reveal the *face* of the battle - that is the external characteristics and features of war; I think that new approaches to the study of the war in the ancient world should consider the *other face* of the battle that is what is behind the fight and lining-up of troops on the battlefield. So according to the recent tendencies of

[*] University of Rome, La Sapienza.

[1] Because of the large quantity of images of war, Assyria has been considered an example of militaristic state: on this definition, see the remarks and reasoning by Fuchs 2005, who finally denies such an interpretation for the Assyrian world and state system.

[2] The list of studies on Assyrian warfare and armies would require too large space: it would be enough to refer to the most recent contributions on the shape and dimension of the Assyrian army (Fales 1990; 2000; 2010; Deszö 2005; 2006; Postgate 2000), the tactics and strategy (De Backer 2007; 2009-2010; Eph'al 2009; Fuchs 2008; 2011; Nadali 2005; 2010; Scurlock 1997), and the political and ideological aspects of warfare (Bahrani 2008; Collins 2014).

[3] On this aspect see the seminal works by Reade 1972; Dalley and Postgate 1984; Dalley 1985.

[4] Nadali and Verderame 2014.

[5] On battering rams (shape and hypothesis of functioning), see Scurlock 1987 and Gillmann 2011.

studying ancient warfare in the Assyrian period, I think we must reflect on what we really know of managing and waging war in ancient Assyria.[6] Of course, our analysis is mainly (let's say exclusively) based on Assyrian sources, both textual and iconographic: we know what the Assyrians tell and show us about their way of waging war in the Near East. The *other face* of the battle should in fact consider all logistical aspects of preparing for war, on one hand, and the reaction of people attacked by the Assyrians, on the other.[7] The careful reading and analysis of the context and content of the correspondence between the Assyrian king and his officials in the provinces of the empire reveals the backstage of the war, describing problems in managing the troops and the necessary food for men and animals, the movement in adverse weather conditions and difficult terrain, the reaction of enemies and the request for supplementary forces, personnel and weapons.[8]

In this respect, it seems to me that Assyrian bas-reliefs hide much more than what they really show about war, since images act a kind of summary of the entire military operation presenting the outcome, reducing the details and even concealing mistakes and failure; although written evidence is never explicit on the failure of the Assyrian war machine,[9] letters can indeed testify particular situations of emergency and problems that are never mentioned in the official inscriptions of the royal annals nor are they carved onto the slabs in the Assyrian palaces. The Assyrian army, according to the image of the palatial bas-reliefs, always wins;[10] it is represented as a solid group of heterogeneous and multi-ethnic men cooperating to achieve a common result. Few pictures depict the preliminary and preparatory stages just before the final attack and conquest of the besieged cities as well as the movement of the troops to reach the next place of the fight.[11]

Due to the nature of the sources at our disposal and because of the modern tendency of considering Assyrian images and inscriptions as the product of a forced propaganda,[12] looking at the *other face* of the battle is of course much more difficult: notwithstanding the real difficulties or impossibilities of gathering data, considerations about strategy and tactics cannot disregard the logistic features that the preparation for a military campaign and a single battle require: according to this principle, the schematic and coded representation of a siege or open field battle

on the Assyrian bas-reliefs should be revaluated taking into consideration the choice of a specific unit of men (infantry, cavalry or chariotry) and the political reasons and impacts of the decision of making (or not making) war by the Assyrian king.[13] I would suggest that studies and research on the ancient warfare (not only in the Assyrian period) should be less technical (thus going beyond the focus on specific fighting techniques and equipment), but should consider all general features of warfare taking into account the two or even the three faces of the battle, that is what occurs before, during and after the fight. In this respect, instead of the history of a single battle or, more specifically, of a single aspect of a battle, we can thus get a history of warfare or a military history including properly military, sociological and economic issues of war: for what concerns the Assyrian world and the amount of information we can gather about war, it is particularly important to confront and cross all kinds of data to enter the meaning and function of war within the Assyrian society, in general, and the institution of kingship, in particular.[14] In the Assyrian time, war had an important and strong economic role since waging war implied the conquest of new territories, the collection of goods and new labour; at the same time, the organisation of a military campaign mobilized people who were in some way attracted by the possibilities of work within and alongside the army as technicians, civilians and part of specialised corps.[15]

Concerning images of war, how can they contribute to the writing of a military history? Assyrian bas-reliefs provide us with the clearest scenes of warfare in the ancient Near East showing details that we can use to describe the technical features of war. But, far from being considered a "catalogue" of items, objects and situations, the aim of a research on Assyrian depictions of war should not simply point to purposely link the scenes with contingent circumstances. Pictures of war have not been created to faithfully represent the reality of wars and fighting (in this respect they are not photos of war);[16] at least, this is not their first and primary intention and in fact they do not show everything, but they omit part of the event. However, it does not mean that Assyrian images of war have been invented and created upon artists' will: on the contrary, pictures of war represent verisimilar actions and operations based on a probable direct presence of

---

[6] Fales 2010; Fuchs 2008 and 2011.

[7] Nadali and Verderame 2014; Nadali 2014.

[8] Fales 2006; Postgate 2000; SAA I 29, 47; V 126, 146, 215; X 175; XI 151, 153-154; XV 14, 136, 280.

[9] Ponchia 1987; Nadali 2009.

[10] Even texts are silent on the failure of the Assyrian army: the Letter to the God Assur of the Assyrian king Sargon II (8th century BC) briefly and laconically reports that "one charioteer, two cavalrymen and three foot-soldiers died", a too small amount to be realistic and that visibly contrasts with the exaggerated hyperbolic numbers of the killed and captured enemies of the official inscriptions (Liverani 2010a: 230).

[11] Nadali 2005: 173-176, 184; Nadali and Verderame 2014: 558.

[12] Liverani 1979; Tadmor 1981 and 1997; Porter 2000; Sano 2016.

[13] See for example the problematic choice in confronting the enemies in an open field battle (Nadali 2010).

[14] Holloway 2002; Vera Chamaza 2005; Bahrani 2008.

[15] Zaccagnini 1983: 260; Nadali and Verderame 2014: 561.

[16] Although details of the landscape and architecture of the enemy cities are so precise that indeed bas-reliefs aim at reproducing the reality of places and spaces (Gunter 1982; Jacoby 1991; Marcus 1995), stories are conditioned by the rules of visual narrative and the physical space of the palace rooms, so that episodes are assembled together in a kind of new and adapted dimension of space and time. In this respect, although based on real events, visual narratives in the Assyrian palaces are properly fictions creating an illusion of the physical space, emphasized and shaped by the volumetric space of the palaces.

artists on the spot.[17] Assyrian bas-reliefs tell military events and episodes that occurred during the military campaign: based on real facts, sculptures rearrange the episodes to transform the *historical* narrative of the war into a *visual historical* narrative for a selected audience within a precise location in the palace. Images of war in the Assyrian palaces have a specific political power intimately tied to the institution of kingship and thus to the person of the king.

If the main audience and recipient of the bas-reliefs in the palace were the Assyrian king and his closest entourage, we can understand and accept why images of war in the Assyrian palaces hide details and concentrate on the culminating moment of the fight and the consequent outcome of the battle with scenes of triumph. The representations of war in the palace are a concrete manifestation of the royal power that is not directed outward:[18] they are part of the foundation of kingship and king's authority and in this specific role one can properly recognize the power of the Assyrian images. Other scenes of war were however depicted outside the palace on steles, obelisks and rock reliefs: if steles and obelisks were clearly visible inside the city in intentional places such as city gates, rock reliefs were on the contrary sculpted in remote places; as a consequence, the meaning of those images is not so strictly linked to the qualities of visibility and accessibility.[19]

If images of war someway hide details of the war, we can even state that they are often "hidden" since they are displayed in non accessible places: taking the bronze bands decorating the gates of temples and palaces into consideration, as the ones made by Assurnasirpal II and Shalmaneser III at Balawat,[20] figures are on so small scale that they cannot be clearly perceived once they are mounted on the wooden door. Again, visibility is not primarily important: it was enough to know that pictures of war and the figure of the king were there regardless if they were perceived and directly seen by the viewers. Indeed, the role of a physical viewer in the flesh seems to be quite irrelevant in this context.

Coming back to what occurs in the Assyrian palaces, scenes of war adorn the core of the royal residence (the throne room) and other rooms permeating the entire architecture of the building, as in the projects of Sargon II, Sennacherib and Assurbanipal.[21] Since war is really the main subject of the sculptures within the Assyrian palaces and architectural spaces are entirely devoted to the celebration of war in pictures, it seems reasonable to speak of an *architecture of war*. The definition does not refer to the architecture and logistic constructions built for military reason: rather it points to the intentional assimilation of war within the architecture of the residence of the Assyrian king according to a project that follows and shares the expansion of the Assyrian empire and the increasing power of the Assyrian king. Indeed, the representation of war inside the palace comes after the outcome of the military campaign of the king; conversely, the presence of the representation of the military deeds of the Assyrian king in his own palace justifies the legitimacy and claim of his augmented power through the elaboration and climax of the royal titulary based on the conquest of new territories and the progressive growing of the empire.[22]

In the palace of Assurnasirpal II, the first comprehensive and elaborated architectural and iconographical project in Assyria, images of war are concentrated in the throne room B and in the West Suite of the palace.[23] The other rooms (East and South Suites around the inner courtyard Y) are decorated with apotropaic deities, palm trees and the majestic pictures of Assurnasirpal II involved in rituals.[24] In the palaces of Sargon II, Sennacherib and Assurbanipal, the throne room and many other rooms are decorated with historical narrative dealing with the royal military campaign. Indeed, the quantity of scenes of warfare is really impressive if compared to other figurative themes: in Sennacherib's palace, except for

---

[17] Madhloom 1970: 121-122; Reade 2012.

[18] At least not specifically and directly: Assyrian bas-reliefs could indeed have been seen publicly, on specific occasions, by a selected group of people, but only temporarily and in the "public" areas of the palaces (external courtyard, throne room). Assurnasirpal II, in the inscription carved on the so-called Banquet Stele (placed in the recess room EA, just outside the eastern gate "c" of the throne room, Russell 1998: fig. 2), celebrates the banquet he organized for 69.574 invited people for the inauguration of his new palace at Nimrud (Grayson 1991: A.0.101.30): at the same time, he states that, once the festival ended, he sent "them back to their lands in peace and joy". Palaces were built by the Assyrian king for their own residence: Assyrian kings clearly state that, while the gods are invited on the occasion of the inauguration of the palace, the building is not a divine residence (Grayson 1991: A.0.87.4 ll. 77-89), but it does represent the place where the kings lives, rules and comes back to after a military campaign (Winter 1993). Nevertheless, because of the magic power Assyrian images had in the construction of the power of the Assyrian kings and because of the sacred nature of the Assyrian kingship (Holloway 2002), gods were the most important, if not the unique, addressees of the message expressed by the bas-reliefs (see now Gillmann 2011-2012).

[19] Moreover, the nature of images is completely different: palace bas-reliefs intend to tell a story, they are a narration of the events; steles, obelisks and rock reliefs, due to the limited figurative space they can offer (particularly steles and obelisks), simply present or refer to a military episode (often recalled in the inscription carved onto the sculpture), without telling it – steles and rock reliefs mainly depict the standing figure of the king as either adoring the gods or subduing the enemy according to recurrent and coded postures. Obelisks display the most significant pictures: the White Obelisk could in fact be considered one of the first attempts of creating a visual narrative that forestalls the later monumentalization of visual narratives under Assurnasirpal II (Pittman 1996). On the other hand, invisibility and inaccessibility of places are the heroic motifs of the Assyrian kings who are able in fact to reach the remotest areas: actually, once the Assyrian king succeeded in reaching such a distant place, he realized that other kings before him achieved the same goal (see for example Feldman 2004; Shafer 2007 and 2014); he finally puts his own image and inscription next to the

previous ones and those places therefore become what we could label as a stratification of (a common shared) memory.

[20] Schachner 2007; Curtis and Tallis 2008.

[21] Reade 1979: 339.

[22] See for example the progress of the conquest and changes of titulary of Sennacherib: Liverani 1981; Nadali 2008.

[23] Kertai 2015: 31-36.

[24] Kertai 2015: 38-41.

Court 6 and room 49 with scenes of transport of the *lamassu*, the sloping passage 51 with the preparation for the banquet and the corridor leading to the Temple of Ishtar,[25] all rooms host the representation of a precise military episode.

In the palace of Assurnasirpal II at Nimrud a distinction between a public and private areas can be recognised and the change of the subject of the sculptures indeed points to this separation; in later residences, war is the pervasive figurative theme of most rooms and a distinction between a public and private areas cannot be based on the subject of sculptures. If we think that the presence of images of war, usually displayed in the throne rooms of each palace, might suggest the open and public nature of the room, we should conversely conclude that the palaces of Sargon II, Sennacherib and Assurbanipal in their totality were accessible and free to people, well beyond the throne room.

But the inner core of the Assyrian palaces was inaccessible, at least for the majority of people, except probably for concessions on very special occasions: therefore, scenes of warfare in the inner rooms of the palaces of Sargon II, Sennacherib and Assurbanipal were almost invisible and unknown to the audience. The situation is similar to what we have previously said about the bronze decoration of the door gates of temples and palaces: scenes of warfare placed in the upper part of the doors (that were approximately 7.92 m high)[26] were impossible to be seen by the viewers who presumably even had difficulties in detecting the nearest bands.[27] The inaccessibility of images is caused by the vertical arrangement of pictures on the total height of the wooden door jambs. Looking at the Assyrian palaces, we can conversely speak of an arrangement of scenes of warfare on the horizontal level going deeper inside the structure of the palace, room by room, farther and farther away from the point of access of the visitor: in the palaces of Sargon II, Sennacherib and Assurbanipal, images of war significantly occupy several rooms of the buildings, even in the spaces that are consistently distant from the courtyard and rooms (the throne room) that are usually considered the only accessed by the "public".

If so, one could logically argue and question why those pictures were projected and shaped if they would have been invisible for the majority of people. Maybe the presence of an audience was not the indispensable requirement for the value of the pictures: it did not give pictures the right to exist. Pictures exist and act irrespective of whether someone looks at them or not. As a consequence, the idea that violent pictures of torture,

killing and devastation are an instrument of the imperial Assyrian propaganda is less convincing and efficacious: in fact, the Assyrian king (as well as the royal family and his loyal entourage) were the only possible direct audience who can have access to all rooms in the palace and thus enjoy all scenes of warfare. And for sure, the Assyrian king had not to be persuasively convinced nor had he suffered his own propaganda: we must thus reconsider the meaning of the Assyrian images of war, even of those showing punishment and cruelties, according to the fruition and location of the sculptures within the palace and the territory of the empire.[28] Rock reliefs, sculpted in remote and difficult places, were not seen except on special ritual occasions: and even in those circumstances, who were the people looking at the pictures? Once again it probably was the king and his closest collaborators, beyond the gods who probably were the first addressees of those remote pictures glorifying the king and his achievements.

Therefore, propaganda is not the main argument and reason to explain the existence of images of war within the Assyrian society:[29] they are much more related to the royal power from an inner point of view. Those images are in fact more directed to king(s) rather than to the Assyrian people and the enemies: the bas-reliefs with narratives of war are in fact placed in the palace, the residence where the king lives and from where he rules the territory of the empire.

The presence of scenes of war inside the residence of the Assyrian kings has no coercive power: the palace is the container of the conquests of the king in space and time and the emphasis on the celebration of the military outcomes by eternalizing the event in sculpture is the base for the construction of the Assyrian memory, kept in one space and built upon past victories to establish the present. As observed by Porada,[30] narrative pictures were expected to influence the future by eternalizing the effect of the enemies' defeat and misery and they were expected to do so acting in the present: according to the Mesopotamian cosmological and chronological conception, in fact, the past was considered to be in front while the future was considered to be behind.[31]

The military outcomes of each Assyrian king stood in front of the successors and those achievements were the foundation of future improvements.

---

[25] Barnett, Bleibtreu and Turner 1998: pls. 78-79, 418-421, 432, 473.
[26] Curtis and Tallis 2015: 60.
[27] The gates were not properly monuments that were supposed to be seen and admired – with visitors standing in front of the open gates looking at the bronze bands – as we are used to doing now in the exhibition in the British Museum (Curtis and Tallis 2015, fig. 1).

[28] On the visibility of cruel images of punishment, see lastly Radner 2015. The question of the visibility, moreover, has a double ramification: on the one hand, it concerns the place where monuments and objects representing violence were physically placed and so when, where and from how many people they could be seen. On the other, it concerns the inner perspective of the images themselves: as an important moment of the narrative of a myth or a battle, violence often defines the culminating act of an event and, for that reason it occupies a dominant role and space.
[29] Gillmann 2011-2012: 205-206.
[30] Porada 1995: 2702-2703.
[31] Liverani 2010b: 52-53.

References

Bahrani, Z. 2008. *Rituals of War: the Body and Violence in Mesopotamia*. Brooklyn.

Barnett, R. D., Bleibtreu, E. and Turner, G. 1998. *Sculptures from the Southwest Palace of Sennacherib at Nineveh*. London.

Collins, P. 2014. Gods, Heroes, Rituals, and Violence: Warfare in Neo-Assyrian Art. In B. A. Brown and M. H. Feldman (eds), *Critical Approaches to Ancient Near Eastern Art*: 619-644. Berlin.

Curtis, J. E. and Tallis, N. (eds) 2008. *The Balawat Gates of Ashur-nasirpal II*. London.

Curtis, J. E. and Tallis, N. 2015. More Thoughts on the Balawat Gates of Shalmaneser III: The Arrangement of the Bands. *Iraq* 77: 59-74.

Dalley, S. 1985. Foreign Chariotry and Cavalry in the Assyrian Armies of Tiglath-pileser III and Sargon II. *Iraq* 47: 31-48.

Dalley, S. and Postgate, J. N. 1984. *The Tablets from Fort Shalmaneser*. London.

De Backer, F. 2007. Some Basic Tactics of Neo-Assyrian Warfare. *Ugarit Forschungen* 39: 69-115.

De Backer, F. 2009-2010. Some Basic Tactics of Neo-Assyrian Warfare 2. Siege Battles. *SAAB* 18: 265-286.

Deszö, T. 2005. The Reconstruction of the Neo-Assyrian Army (as Depicted on the Assyrian Palace Reliefs, 745-612 BC). *Acta Archaeologica Academiae Scientiarum Hungaricae* 57: 87-130.

Deszö, T. 2006. Reconstrcution of the Assyrian Army of Sargon II (721-705 B.C.), Based on the Nimrud Horse Lists. *SAAB* 15: 93-140.

Eph'al, I. 2009. *The City Besieged. Siege and Its Manifestations in the Ancient Near East*, CHANE 36. Leiden.

Fales, F. M. 1990. Grain Reserves, Daily Rations, and the Size of the Assyrian Army. *SAAB* 4: 3-34.

Fales, F. M. 2000. Preparing for War in Assyria. In J. Andreau, P. Briant and R. Descat (eds), *Économie antique. La guerre dans les économies antiques*, Entretiens d'Archéologie et d'Histoire III: 35-62. St.-Bertrand-de-Comminges.

Fales, F. M. 2006. Cibare i deportati. Una lettera al re assiro Tiglath-Pileser III (ND 2634). In D. Morandi Bonacossi *et al.* (eds), *Tra Oriente e Occidente. Studi in onore di Elena Di Filippo Balestrazzi*: 47-64. Padova.

Fales, F. M. 2010. *Guerre et paix en Assyrie. Religion et imperialism*. Paris.

Feldman, M. H. 2004. Nineveh to Thebes and Back: Art and Politics between Assyria and Egypt in the Seventh Century BCE. *Iraq* 66: 141-150.

Fuchs, A. 2005. War das Neuassyrisches Reich ein Militärstaat? In B. Meißner, O. Schmitt and M. Sommer (eds), *Krieg – Gesellschaft – Institutionen. Beiträge zu einer vergleichenden Kriegsgeschichte*: 35-60. Berlin.

Fuchs, A. 2008. Über den Wert von Befestigungsanlagen. *ZA* 98: 45-99.

Fuchs, A. 2011. Assyria at War: Strategy and Conduct. In K. Radner and E. Robson (eds), *The Oxford Handbook of Cuneiform Culture*: 380-401. Oxford.

Gillmann, N. 2011. Les tortues neo-assyriennes. *Historiae* 8: 31-64.

Gillmann, N. 2011-2012. Les bas-reliefs néo-assyriens: une nouvelle tentative d'interprétation. *SAAB* 19: 203-237.

Grayson, A. K. 1991. *Assyrian Rulers of the Early First Millennium BC (1114-859 BC)*, RIMA 2. Toronto.

Gunter, A. 1982. Representations of Urartian and Western Iranian Fortress Architecture in the Assyrian Reliefs. *Iran* 20: 103-112.

Holloway, S. W. 2002. *Aššur is King! Aššur is King*, CHANE 10. Leiden.

Jacoby, R. 1991. The Representation and Identification of Cities on Assyrian Reliefs. *Israel Exploration Journal* 41: 112-131.

Kertai, D. 2015. *The Architecture of Late Assyrian Royal Palaces*. Oxford.

Liverani, M. 1979. Ideology of the Assyrian Empire. In M. T. Larsen (ed), *Power and Propaganda: A Symposium on Ancient Empires*, Mesopotamia 7: 297-317. Copenhagen.

Liverani, M. 1981. Critique of Variants and the Titulary of Sennacherib. In F. M. Fales (ed), *Assyrian Royal Inscriptions: New Horizons in Literary, Ideological, and Historical Analysis. Papers of a Symposium held in Cetona (Siena), June 26-28 1980*: 225-257. Roma.

Liverani, M. 2010. 'Untruthful Steles': Propaganda and Reliability in Ancient Mesopotamia. In S. C. Melville and A. L. Slotsky (eds), *Opening the Tablet Box. Near Eastern Studies in Honor of Benjamin R. Foster*, CHANE 42: 229-244. Leiden.

Liverani, M. 2010b. Parole di bronzo, di pietra, d'argilla. *Scienze dell'Antichità* 16: 27-62.

Madhloom, T. 1970. *The Chronological Development of Neo-Assyrian Art*. London.

Marcus, M. I. 1987. Geography as an Organization Principle in the Imperial Art of Shalmaneser III. *Iraq* 49: 77-90.

Nadali, D. 2005. Assyrians to War: Positions, Patterns and Canons in the Tactics of the Assyrian Armies in the VII Century BC. In A. Di Ludovico and D. Nadali (eds), *Studi in onore di Paolo Matthiae presentati in occasione del suo sessantacinquesimo compleanno*, CMAO 10: 167-207. Roma.

Nadali, D. 2008. The Role of the Image of the King in the Organizational and Compositional Principles of Sennacherib's Throne Room: A Guide to the Historical Narrative and Meaning of a Specified Message. In H. Kühne, R. M. Czichon and F. J. Kreppner (eds), *Proceedings of the 4th International Congress on the Archaeology of the Ancient Near East 29 March-3 April 2004, Freie Universität Berlin. Volume 1: The Reconstruction of Environment: Natural Resources and Human Interrelations through Time Art History: Visual Communication*: 473-493. Berlin.

Nadali, D. 2009. Sieges and Similes of Sieges in the Royal Annals: The Conquest of Damascus by Tiglath-Pileser III. *KASKAL* 6: 137-149.

Nadali, D. 2010. Assyrian Open Field Battles. An Attempt at Reconstruction and Analysis. In J. Vidal (ed) *Studies on War in the Ancient Near East. Collected Essays on Military History*, AOAT 372: 117-152. Münster.

Nadali D. 2014. The Impact of War of Civilians in the Neo-Assyrian Period. In D. Nadali and J. Vidal (eds), *The Other Face of the Battle. The Impact of War on Civilians in the Ancient Near East* AOAT 413: 101-111. Münster.

Nadali D. and Verderame L. 2014. Experts at War Masters Behind the Ranks of the Assyrian Army. In H. Neumann *et al.* (eds) *Krieg und Frieden im Alten Vorderasien. 52e Rencontre Assyriologique Internationale, International Congress of Assyriology and Near Eastern Archaeology, Münster, 17.-21. Juli 2006*, AOAT 401: 553-566. Münster.

Pittman, H. 1996. The White Obelisk and the Problem of Historical Narrative in the Art of Assyria. *The Art Bulletin* 78: 334-355.

Ponchia, S. 1987. Analogie, metafore e similitudini nelle iscrizioni reali assire: semantica e ideologia. *Oriens antiquus* 26: 223-255.

Porada, E. 1995. Understanding Ancient Near Eastern Art: a Personal Account. In J. M. Sasson (ed), *Civilizations of the Ancient Near East*, Vol. IV: 2695-2714. New York.

Porter, B. N. 2000. Assyrian Propaganda for the West. Esarhaddon's Stelae for Til Barsip and Sam'al. In G. Bunnes (ed) *Essays on Syria in the Iron Age*, ANES Supplement 7: 143-176. Louvain.

Postgate, J. N. 2000. The Assyrian Army in Zamua. *Iraq* 62: 89-108.

Radner, K. 2015. High Visibility Punishment and Deterrent: Impalement in Assyrian Warfare and Legal Practice. *Zeitschrift für Altorientalische und Biblische Rechtsgeschichte* 21: 103-128.

Reade, J. E. 1972. The Neo-Assyrian Court and Army: Evidence from the Sculptures. *Iraq* 34: 87-112.

Reade, J. E. 1979. Ideology and Propaganda in Assyrian Art. In M. T. Larsen (ed) *Power and Propaganda. A Symposium on Ancient Empires*, Mesopotamia 7: 329-343. Copenhagen.

Reade, J. E. 2012. Visual Evidence for the Status and Activities of Assyrian Scribes. In G. B. Lanfranchi *et al.* (eds) *Leggo! Studies Presented to Frederick Mario Fales on the Occasion of His 65th Birthday*, Wiesbaden, 699-717.

Russell, J. M. 1998. The Program of the Palace of Assurnasirpal II at Nimrud: Issues in the Research and Presentation of Assyrian Art. *American Journal of Archaeology* 102/4: 655-715.

Sano, K. 2016. Die Repräsentation der Königsherrschaft in neuassyrischer Zeit: Ideologie, Propaganda und Adressaten der Königsinschriften. *StMes* 3: 215-236.

Schachner, A. 2007. *Bilder eines Weltreichs. Kunst- und kultur-geschichtliche Untersuchungen zu den Verzierungen eines Tores aus Balawat (Imgur-Enlil) aus der Zeit von Salmanassar III, König von Assyrien*, Subartu 20. Turnhout.

Scurlock, J. 1987. Assyrian Battering Rams Revisited, *SAAB* 3/2: 129-131.

Scurlock, J. 1997. Neo-Assyrian Battle Tactics. In G. D. Young, M. W. Chavalas and R. E. Averbeck (eds) *Crossing Boundaries and Linking Horizons. Studies in Honor of Michael C. Astour on His 80th Birthday*: 491-517. Bethesda.

Shafer, A. 2007. Assyrian Royal Monuments on the Periphery: Ritual and the Making of Imperial Space. In J. Cheng and M. H. Feldman (eds) *Ancient Near Eastern Art in Context: Studies in Honor of Irene J. Winter by Her Students*, CHANE 26: 133-159.

Shafer, A. 2014. The Assyrian Landscape as Ritual. In B. A. Brown and M. H. Feldman (eds) *Critical Approaches to Ancient Near Eastern Art*: 713-739. Berlin.

Tadmor, H. 1981. History and Ideology in the Assyrian Royal Inscriptions. In F. M. Fales (ed) *Assyrian Royal Inscriptions: New Horizons in Literary, Ideological, and Historical Analysis. Papers of a Symposium held in Cetona (Siena) June 26–28, 1980*: 13-33. Roma.

Tadmor, H. 1997. Propaganda, Literature, Historiography. Cracking the Code of the Assyrian Royal Inscriptions. In S. Parpola, R. M. Whiting (eds), *Assyria 1995. Proceedings of the 10th Anniversary Symposium of the Neo-Assyrian Text Corpus Project, Helsinki, September 7-11, 1995*: 325-338. Helsinki.

Vera Chamaza, G. W. 2006. *Die Omnipotenz Aššurs: Entwicklungen in der Aššur-Theologie unter den Sargoniden Sargon II, Sanherib und Asarhaddon*, AOAT 295. Münster.

Winter, I. J. 1993. 'Seat of Kingship'/ "A Wonder to Behold": The Palace as Construct in the Ancient Near East. *Ars Orientalis* 23: 27-55.

Zaccagnini, C. 1983. Patterns of Mobility among Ancient Near Eastern Craftsmen. *JNES* 42: 247-249.